In
Search
of Shipwrecks

In
Search
of Shipwrecks

Jim Jenney

For Ray Kenneth,
With Best Regards!
Jim Jenney

South Brunswick and New York: A. S. Barnes and Company
London: Thomas Yoseloff Ltd

© 1980 by A. S. Barnes and Co., Inc.

A. S. Barnes and Co., Inc.
Cranbury, New Jersey 08512

Thomas Yoseloff Ltd
Magdalen House
136-148 Tooley Street
London SE1 2TT, England

Library of Congress Cataloging in Publication Data

Jenney, Jim.
   In search of shipwrecks.

   Includes index.
   1. Treasure-trove. 2. Shipwrecks—New England.
I. Title.
G525.J46   917.4   78-75312
ISBN 0-498-02389-0

PRINTED IN THE UNITED STATES OF AMERICA

Contents

In
Search
of Shipwrecks

PART I

PREFACE

Wreck searching is an art—one which requires that several basic prereq-
uisites be well understood. Part I is a summary of the techniques and tools
necessary to start your search correctly and to lead you on the best
possible path to its successful conclusion. The portion of this first section
devoted to researching may seem at the outset to be somewhat dry but it is
upon this foundation that your success will entirely depend. The chapter
concerning the tools and other equipment needed for your search is
merely suggestive of what you might try and by no means is a sum total of
all available tools which can be adapted to your searching. The search
techniques discussed are those which we have found to be the most
helpful in our searches and other techniques, particularly on-the-spot
techniques, may often be required in the variety of situations that you
will face in your quest. The chapter on artifacts is fairly complete and up
to date as to today's most commonly used preservative methods but,
again, do not put your complete faith in only one methodology. The
most important trick, if there is a trick to wreck searching, is to use
everything you have—including your head!—when dealing with the
various situations that will inevitably arise in your search.

1 Research

WHEN a scuba diver first becomes interested in searching for shipwrecks he generally envisions himself gliding serenely through crystal clear water and suddenly finding himself face to face with an intact ship, whether an old Spanish brig or a modern tanker, simply sitting on the bottom upright looking just as it looked on the day it was launched. It becomes apparent as the wreck diver gains experience that this is simply not the case (with some notable exceptions). In the first place, very few divers ever have the good fortune to discover a wreck by accident, to say nothing of the fact that crystal clear water does not exist universally in all oceans. The art of wreck searching involves many time consuming techniques; often, sophisticated equipment is employed in the diver's search. The method of search most effectively used by the most successful wreck hunters includes many hours of research followed by an organized physical search of the area in which the wreck *should* be located. Many times a wreck will be located where it shouldn't be, however, and this is part of the challenge which makes the successful culmination of a wreck search so fantastically enjoyable. To begin at the beginning involves a study of basic research sources and the formation of a technique.

A basic rule to follow before you attempt to locate any shipwreck is to know what you are looking for. This requires a basic knowledge of ship types and construction in general. There are several books which deal with ship construction and perhaps the best general reference that I have found is *The Lore of Ships*, by Tre Tryckare. Once you have acquired a little background in ship construction it will become readily apparent that objects such as a cutlass bearing and a deadeye are probably not from the same vessel, and a motorized winch would not be found in the remains of a Spanish brig of 18th century vintage. These facts will be of great importance when the time comes to identify your wreck when another may lie in the same general area. When the diver has become basically familiar with ship construction and types he must then make his first important decision: "What kind of shipwreck do I want to find?" Every diver's interest will vary as to what he wants to find. Some will be interested only in 18th century sailing vessels while others will be interested in early wooden steam vessels or perhaps a modern freighter. This decision will affect the researcher diver greatly in the type of source material he seeks. There are several basic sources of wreck research material available and each will be discussed in some detail as to where it can be obtained, what information it will yield and to what type of shipwreck it will be most pertinent.

By far the largest single source of information available concerning shipwrecks in general would be the United States National Archives located in Washington, D.C. Reports from several governmental agencies which refer to wrecks can be found here and they must each be mentioned as to their nature and usefulness.

The United States Life Saving Service—The Life Saving Service was the forerunner of today's United States Coast Guard and from its formation in 1872 until it was reformulated as the Coast Guard in 1915 it maintained a fairly accurate and well organized set of records covering the activities of every Life Saving Service District throughout the United States. It was the duty of each station to keep a log of all activities relative to the saving of life and limb from shipwrecks and related disasters. This is one of the better early sources of information concerning marine disasters but it must be remembered that the log referred only to incidents in which the men of the station were involved and that these stations were located at only the most dangerous points along the coast: they might be ten miles or more apart. This would leave more than enough room for a shipwreck to occur between two stations unnoticed and probably unaided. There is nothing to say that a wreck has to occur on the most dangerous section of the coast and, in fact, in many cases they have occurred in very unlikely areas. This is a major weakness of the Life Saving Service Reports, but it is balanced by its strong points.

The information in their annual reports was set up chronologically for each district and gives the researcher the following facts if known: date of the disaster; name, type and nationality of the vessel; the station involved and locality of the disaster; and the nature of the casualty and the service rendered by the men of the station. The information is easily readable and usually concise and often mentions facts of great importance which may bring your search for a particular vessel to a rapid conclusion. For an example, within the Third Life Saving District for the year 1898 the following account is found: "November 27; Scs. Ira & Abbie, and

Arabell; Block Island, Rhode Island; These two schooners together with several small boats, went ashore during the hurricane, and the surfmen could do nothing at the time to save them. Three men from the Ira & Abbie were succored at the station, and on the 28th the surfmen attempted to float the Arabell. The attempt was not successful, however, and the Keeper advised the Master to hire a tug, which was done, and the schooner was saved. The Ira & Abbie was also eventually floated." The last short and simple statement referring to the Ira & Abbie saved me considerable time in further researching into the fate of this vessel as she actually remained on the beach more than a week before she was floated. As time passed, the life saving aspect of the service became less vital while the service as a whole became increasingly complex until it eventually came under the control of the military forces and became known as the United States Coast Guard.

The United States Coast Guard—In the initial years of its growth the Coast Guard followed the pattern of the former service with regard to its reports relating to marine disasters but with the increasing use of motor powered vessels over sailing vessels and through a continually improving standard of aids to navigation the interest in accurate records relating to the shipwrecks themselves dwindled. By the early 1920s the annual report of the Coast Guard had diminished to a fraction of its former size and now dealt more with problems of the budget than anything else. The earlier annual reports of the Coast Guard have much interesting material relating to the number and types of vessels lost and cover a much broader geographical area than did the former service. An interesting phenomenon had begun to take shape about this time which relates directly to wrecks of this vintage. Many times a vessel when sailing offshore encountered a severe storm and would be abandoned by its crew but would not sink, with the result that many vessels which were listed as being lost at sea actually became floating derelicts which wandered at the whim of the wind and currents in the open ocean. Care is necessary when you are dealing with a stranded vessel of this period which is reported as having broken up within one or two days; in actuality it may have worked its way off shore and joined the ranks of the derelicts. This happened surprisingly often. Among the major improvements in the aids to navigation at this time were the lighthouses which were initially controlled by the United States Lighthouse Service, another important source of shipwreck information.

The United States Lighthouse Service—The U.S. Lighthouse Service was one of the earliest formed government agencies. As did all governmental agencies, it kept records of services rendered and events of interest which took place within its jurisdiction. Obviously, the information that is of greatest interest to us as wreck searchers is that pertinent to the loss of vessels. Lighthouses were usually located at the most dangerous points along the coast in order to prevent such disasters by ships, particularly those sailing at night, but in the era of primitive lighthouses when a captain's decision to use dead reckoning predominated over using the other aids, many a captain came to grief because his instincts told him that the lighthouse he spotted was, say, the Point Judith Light around which he could safely navigate to southward when, in fact, it was the lighthouse at Sandy Point, Block Island, only seven miles away, and in passing to the south he would sail into the desolate and rocky shore of Block Island. Such navigational errors were not uncommon before the modern advances of electric lamps in lighthouses, radio, LORAN, and other electronic aids to navigation. So in fact many shipwrecks occurred in the vicinity of early lighthouses. As a source of information the annual reports of the Lighthouse Service give the researcher an accurate date but little else of importance to him. When the night was clear it would be possible for the keeper of the light to give a description as to the size and rig of the vessel in distress and also a fairly accurate location as to the disaster but most shipwrecks occurring at night were very hard to describe or even exactly locate and the name of the distressed vessel could only be gained from a survivor, if there were any survivors. Getting away from sailing vessels for a moment, a comprehensive source of information concerning wrecks of steam vessels is the reports of the United States Steamboat Inspection Service.

United States Steamboat Inspection Service—As a method of reducing marine disasters to steam vessels the U.S. Steamboat Inspection Service was created during the latter decades of the 19th century. Early steam vessels often had short lives due generally to the worst possible accident for a mariner—fire. The earliest steamboats, dating from as early as 1815, burned wood for fuel and sparks from the furnaces were cause for more than one major disaster. With the increased use of coal for fuel this problem was much reduced but by no means eliminated. Steamers were also quite subject to demise from collisions as the steamship lines competed fiercely in the attempt to run the shortest possible time from port to port. At night and in the fog this often proved to be a fatal race for both the owners and their vessels. The function of the Steamboat Inspection Service was to see that the vessels were sound for the distances they would have to travel and to see that proper safety equipment was available to keep the possibility of loss of life at a minimum level. Their records include losses of vessels and any and all pertinent information regarding such losses. For researchers interested in early steam vessels this source of research information is invaluable. If modern vessels are your interest another good source of information from the National Archives is the annual report of Merchant Vessels of the United States.

Merchant Vessels of the United States—The annual report *Merchant Vessels of the United States* has always been a fine source of information concerning large merchant vessels belonging to the United States. It is broken down into several sections and contains much valuable technical information concerning the size, power, and description of merchant vessels which, during any particular year, are sailing the coastal waters of the United States or are in international waters. Also, within this annual report is any available information concerning vessels lost in that particular year. The information offered is usually: date, location (often in longitude and latitude), and the cargo, as well as the other particulars mentioned above.

This very briefly summarizes the information available to the student of shipwreck research through the National Archives. It is the largest source by volume of material that the researcher has access to and it is here that his search will probably begin. There are several other fine sources of basic information that we shall explore further.

The second major source of information concerning shipwrecks of all sizes and descriptions is marine insurance companies. Almost all major merchant vessels now and even during the early days of marine shipping carried some amount of insurance either on the vessel or on the cargo, if not both. Probably the largest marine insurance company in the world is Lloyd's, a British insurance firm with a very long and reputable history. Even as early as the 18th century Lloyds was very well known in the business as being willing to insure almost anything. Their records keeping capacity was immense even when the total volume of shipping was miniscule in relation to modern day super cargo ships and tankers. *The Lloyd's Register of Shipping* was an annual publication somewhat similar to *Merchant Vessels of the United States* but on a tremendously larger scale as Lloyd's insured vessels from nearly every country in the world. A modern *Lloyd's Register* is broken down into several sections by type of vessel—sailing vessel *vs* power vessel—and the power vessels are further subdivided as to whether they are less than or greater than 300 tons. The technical information offered within these registers is generally more detailed than that in the *Merchant Vessels* publication but basically is of the same variety. You may have some difficulty in locating these records to do research from but they are well worth the trouble to find.

Very closely related to the marine insurance companies is the information obtainable from professional salvage and wrecking companies. One of the larger and older salvage companies on the east coast was Scott Wrecking which later became Merritt, Chapman, and Scott. The information available from these companies may also be hard to come by but if obtainable it is more than worthwhile. Keep in mind when you have an interest in wrecks that in the early days of the 19th century mariners were very unwilling to give up to the sea anything which might even remotely be salvageable and often years were spent in semi-successful salvage attempts. An interesting example of this came from a series of letters dated 1815 about a diver named Bailey Brooks who, using a diving bell, recovered hundreds of anchors, chains, rigging, etc. from wrecks lost in New England waters. Persistence for him and others has paid off in the past as well as in the present and although this serves only to diminish your chances for locating a virgin shipwreck, never fear—they do still exist!

Another form of wrecker also provides us with a good source of information. This wrecker is the United States Army Corps of Engineers, one of whose tasks it is to destory obstructions to navigation. Very often a wreck would occur at the entrance to a harbor in relatively shallow water and this pile of ship's bones would present a problem to other vessels entering the same port. The danger here was significantly more important if the vessel's remains were not visible at the surface but lay under just a few feet of water and became an invisible menace. Whenever such a situation was discovered the Corps of Engineers was immediately called in to destroy or remove the vessel's remains so that another vessel would not be endangered by the hazard. The engineers of the Corps are not professional salvagers, however, and a wreck which they have destroyed usually retains all its parts—although usually spread out over a large area.

It was necessary for the Corps to retain a record of where their funds were used in order for them to secure further federal funds. Also, signed reports were often required as to the success of their demolition to insure the safety of future vessels in the vicinity of removed obstructions. These reports can sometimes be located and yield accurate facts of importance to wreck searchers. In addition to these reports, at certain times wreck charts (particularly of the waters around major ports) were published which indicated the locations of many wrecked vessels. The key to one wreck chart of the Third Life Saving District lists over 1,000 wrecked vessels. The information in this key is fairly detailed: date of disaster, location, name and type of ship, and type of disaster (wrecked, collision, foundered, sunk, lost at sea, etc.). When available from the nearest district office of the Corps of Engineers the information concerning their removal of obstructions can be quite helpful in your search.

Maritime museums and libraries usually open their doors to the dedicated researcher. Almost every major port offers some type of maritime museum and several in this country are of particular importance in terms of the information they have on hand. Peabody Museum in Salem, Massachusetts has some of the finest information obtainable anywhere and will allow a researcher to use its facilities. Among the most helpful bits of information held in this repository are innumerable photographs of ships of all ages, sizes, and types. Mystic Seaport in Mystic, Connecticut is another exceptional institution available to the researcher. Not only do they have a photographic file (similar to that at Peabody Museum) but they also have a large research library which includes many of the sources of information mentioned as being available from the National Archives. They have the Life Saving Service records and even the records of at least one of the early wrecking companies. Along with the research facilities located there, Old Mystic Seaport offers the researcher the chance to see a typical seaport village in some detail and maintained as it was in the 19th century. They also have an intact whaleship, the Charles W. Morgan, for the student of early ship construction. Truly, this is a fine source of many different types of applicable shipping research and memorabilia. Further south is the Mariners Museum of Newport News, Virginia. This is perhaps the finest source of information relating to government owned vessels in the entire United States. Here, as in the other two maritime museums mentioned, is a repository of ship photographs spanning a period of many decades and including both sailing and powered vessels. These maritime museums along with many others provide the researcher with a source of many different types of information, probably the most important being the photographic files. Given the opportunity to view a picture of a sought after wreck before the search begins the wreck searcher has an edge in knowing exactly what he is looking for. On a smaller scale than sophisticated marine museums but perhaps more important for other reasons to be mentioned are the next sources of information—local historical societies.

Local historical societies are the final step for the wreck researcher. No matter how much general information he has acquired from the prior sources he will obtain his final information for this source. With the basics of the ship's construction in mind (which can be gathered from the general sources of research mentioned) the more difficult task is in determining the exact location of the vessel's remains. If the vessel is not of very early vintage (18th or 19th century) it may be possible to find someone who either remembers seeing the disaster or was involved with the salvage efforts or at best may even have been aboard the vessel when disaster struck. This can usually be done with the greatest success at the nearest locality to the site of the disaster. Almost every port has some sort of historical repository; information available here can be in the form of local records, photographs (perhaps of the disaster itself), and newspaper accounts. Newspaper accounts will be discussed separately as they have significant importance in their own right but the point is clear that local sources of information, particularly historical societies, can be an invaluable aid to the wreck searcher. Not to be overlooked are the specialized historical societies whose members dwell on a specific interest and acquire much detailed information concerning this interest. A fine example is the Steamship Historical Society of America whose members have compiled countless pages of documentation and thousands of photographs relating solely to North American steamships. For steamship hunters the information from this fine source is an essential ingredient to a successful search. Another source of information to be mentioned is books.

Books as a source of shipwreck information fall into two categories: 1) those written at the time of the disaster; and 2) those written in modern times concerning historical marine disasters. There are advantages and disadvantages to both which should briefly be mentioned. With an old book the facts of the disaster are apt to be more precise because of the nearness of the actual disaster to the date of the book but these accounts may be somewhat undecipherable as the style of writing in many early books was very flowery and often emphasized the deeds of the life savers or crew of the vessel in distress while leaving out the details most pertinent to wreck searchers as to the location of the wreck. Modern books often suffer from the opposite problem: they are quite easy to read but rarely precise. As a general rule, use a good deal of caution in relying on information derived from a book.

These are your basic research sources. They will all lead you to the final source of information to look into before you actually start your physical search—the newspaper accounts.

The local newspaper is always the best source for information relating to the exact location of your shipwrecked vessel. The key to this preceding sentence is the word local. A town located ten or fifteen miles from the vicinity of the wreck may have a newspaper with reasonably good accounts of the disaster but a more local newspaper will always have the best of all possible accounts to be gathered. Almost all port cities in which any amount of trade was carried on had in their papers a daily account entitled "Marine Intelligence" or "Marine List" in which would be found items of interest to mariners and shipowners, including disasters to vessels, changes in navigational aids, and correspondence between vessels on lengthy voyages brought home by passing vessels. When a local marine disaster occurred there would normally be a detailed account of the disaster in the general news columns and these accounts would usually continue daily if the vessel did not break up immediately. The accounts would follow the progress of salvage attempts until the wreck was sold at auction as she lay, pulled off, or was destroyed by the severe conditions of wind and sea. One of the few problems that may arise here is concerning the names of places, particularly rocks and reefs, whose name may have been changed over the years leaving no hint as to where the shipwreck occurred. A good example in my research was a rock first known as the "Washbowl." Originally, this area was probably named for its frothy white water which is quite similar to that found in a wash bowl but why was its name later changed to Butler's Bull Rock and still later Butterball Rock? This gives you some insight into the possible problems that you can come across when dealing with early wrecks if you don't know the local names of today and yesteryear well. The easiest way to surmount this problem is to study as many early charts of your area as possible and make note of name changes for further reference. Local historical societies will usually have the early charts to refer to.

One thing that you must learn to do is to read the old newspaper accounts with a careful eye. Although they were never written to be deceptive or tricky many newspaper accounts ramble, contradict themselves, and in general can confuse the shipwreck researcher until he gains experience and "gets the feel" of interpreting them. Particularly in the earliest accounts the reporter tended to put his emphasis on the efforts of man to save his fellow man or to save himself and often it is frustrating to find that the information concerning the disaster itself is very brief. When you have gathered and studied these accounts you are only one step away from beginning your physical search.

Once the general area has been determined there is one final step to be taken before the diving actually begins—making up a sketch of the general area with a grid pattern for reference. In setting up this grid you should work from the center of the general area to the edges of this area making the squares of an equal size (probably about twenty feet square to start). As your search progresses you can mark off the areas that you eliminate as not having any remains. This will be discussed in greater detail later with searching techniques.

One final aspect of research must be mentioned to complete a discussion of this all-important first phase of wreck searching—correspondence and correspondents. Needless to say, all of us who are interested in wreck searching cannot afford the time nor the money to just drop in at the National Archives in Washington or to visit Mystic Seaport or Peabody Museum. For just this reason man invented the pencil, paper, envelope and stamp. In truth, correspondence is an essential tool to the researcher and when dealing with other researchers or historical societies I have had very good results with such correspondence. As an example, I recently mailed out a questionnaire regarding vessels lost in the Portland Gale of November 27, 1898, to approximately one hundred twenty five sources and received more than one hundred and fifteen responses, many with very useful information. As your name becomes more familiar to other researchers you will find that they are very helpful indeed and ask of you only that you might aid them in their research should you come across information that would be helpful to them. All in all, your correspondents may be your most valuable sources of information to be found.

With a basic understanding of research sources and techniques firmly in hand we are now ready to enter the water to search for our shipwreck. There are some basic tools that will be necessary for the physical search and for the recovery of artifacts. These will be discussed in some detail in the next chapter.

2 Equipment and Tools

T HERE are very few, if any, fields of endeavor today in which tools of some sort are not essential and the art of wreck searching is definitely no exception to the standard rule. The tools necessary in a search for shipwrecks are actually only one segment of the overall equipment needed for a complete program of locating, working on, and recovering artifacts from a shipwreck. The major determining factor to the wreck searcher in his choice of tools and equipment is his budget. Although a very sophisticated project may involve thousands of dollars worth of equipment it is possible to carry out a smaller scale project for a fraction of that cost. In discussing the types of equipment for a complete project there are three categories into which this equipment falls logically: 1) equipment necessary to locate the wrecksite; 2) tools necessary to work in the remains; and 3) equipment necessary for the retrieval of artifacts.

The equipment necessary to locate the wrecksite will vary with the type of wreck sought, whether a shallow water wreck or a deep water wreck. The basic difference between these two types of wrecks in relation to your equipment necessary for locating the wrecksite is, generally, whether or not you will be using a boat or diving from shore. Ideally, your wrecksite would be close to shore but lie in water of forty foot of depth or greater. This situation is rare, however, and it must be stated here that probably the best wrecks lie in deeper water. Shallow water wrecks are generally spread out over a large area and are subject, by the action of the sea, to being very broken up and have a great deal of camouflage from kelp and calcareous growth. Deep water wrecks (forty to eighty foot depth) are generally much more intact as they are less subject to the action of the waves but again are subject to the camouflaging growth of seaweeds. The tools necessary to work on a shallow water wreck from shore are simply your personal diving equipment coupled with the techniques of free-swimming search and circle search to be discussed later.

The tools necessary to locate a deepwater or offshore wreck begin with a boat. This is where your budget comes into play. If your budget will allow it a large inboard-powered vessel with facilities for several days or weeks stay is the most convenient working platform for your searching party. The advantages here are almost too numerous to mention including an onboard compressor, large capacity for sophisticated electronics equipment, sleeping facilities, long range capability and hauling and storage capacity for artifacts. That is a fine system if you can afford it financially and you have the time to devote to the task but a more realistic small scale operation can be utilized as well at much less expense. A small boat (up to twenty feet in length) with an outboard motor can be a most effective tool for both shallow and deep water searching. It has the advantages of maneuverability and economy with the basic loss of luxury and carrying capacity only and, if trailerable, a small boat can almost meet the range of a larger vessel although limited to an offshore distance of perhaps five miles.

To equip your boat, whether large or small, your budget again comes into play. Electronic equipment used for the location of objects on the ocean floor can be expensive but careful shopping and experience with a small boat can be almost as effective as a large vessel complete with full electronics. A fathometer or depth recorder is an essential piece of electronics for any craft searching for shipwreck remains. These can be found in two basic varieties—a graph recorder type which draws a bottom profile on graph paper and the non-recorder type which may be as accurate but requires the constant attention of one member of the searching team. With some practice a viewer of a non-recording fathometer can learn to distinguish between the false echo of a school of fish and a wreck (or rock) and even between different types of bottom composition.

Probably the most popular second piece of electronics gear which goes beyond the range of the economy minded wreck searcher is side-scan sonar. This is another echo returning type of electronic equipment which draws a graph of an angled view of the bottom making it possible to search a much larger area of bottom in a shorter period of time. I have had the opportunity to see a side scan unit pick up a wreck while ten miles off shore within ten minutes after the general area was reached. It is very effective! This is generally the best unit to use in conjunction with a fathometer particularly in an area where the bottom is fairly flat with few or only small rocks.

Another very expensive and very useful piece of electronic gear is a LORAN unit (Long Range Aid to Navigation). The principal behind LORAN is the pinpoint triangulation of a spot through signals sent from stations located at different points on shore. This is probably the most accurate way to pinpoint your location while at sea but in order to use it effectively for wreck searching you must know the exact point at which your wreck lies. Therefore, it is used more perhaps for returning to a previously located wreck which you have found, and decide not to mark with a buoy, and will provide accuracy to within about one hundred feet of the spot.

One final piece of electronic gear to mention has only recently come into popularity as a wreck locating tool, namely, a magnetometer or metal detector. Very simply, a magnetometer measures fluctuations in the earth's magnetic field caused by large masses of metal. The theory behind the use of a magnetometer for wreck searching is that almost all ships, including very early sailing vessels, carried a great deal of metal aboard (whether in the form of cannon or as a hull material or fittings) and by towing a submersible magnetometer in the area of a wrecked vessel you may learn its location by the large metal deposits in that area which hopefully indicate the ship's remains. The obvious disadvantage of using a magnetometer is that it does not discriminate between a pile of junk on the bottom and the remains of a shipwreck. However, the magnetometer has gained increased popularity of late and has proven itself a worthy tool.

There are several other tools that are useful to the wreck searcher in locating his prize which are not in the category of electronic equipment and are well within the range of the small scale wreck searcher. To begin a search of the general area in which your wreck should be located I have mentioned the use of a grid system. When at sea an effective method that has been used to set up a grid involves buoying off the general area in a square or rectangular pattern. To do this you will need at least six buoys, line for each of them, and weights for anchoring them. For buoys Clorox bottles will suffice (although for visibility in a heavy sea a larger buoy with a flag on it may be necessary) which can be painted or otherwise. Line can be purchased or if you are enterprising you may pick up line from old broken-up lobster pots on the bottom if this line is in good condition. You will need a considerable amount of line in varying lengths and I have found a system which works well and uses a minimum amount of line. Utilizing fifty-foot sections of line with an eye splice at one end and a clip at the other end provides you with line that can be varied in length easily while on the site and stores well in your rope locker.

Normally, ten to twenty sections of line should be carried to allow for setting up to ten buoys in ninety feet of water. For weighting the buoys it is easy enough to make a few dives and pick up lost sinkers on the bottom. By melting them down and using discarded soup or vegetable cans for a mold you will end up with seven to ten pound weights which are just right in most conditions. Once you have set up your general grid pattern another tool comes into play to help make your search more efficient.

Useful to a depth of about sixty feet, an underwater towing sled is perhaps one of the wreck searcher's most important tools. These sleds or planing boards are extremely easy to construct and offer the wreck diver an immense advantage over the free swimming searcher in terms of area covered, time in the water (air consumption is much reduced) and overall efficiency. They also provide an advantage over electronics in that the diver can see exactly what is the object at hand whereas electronic equipment simply indicate a large unknown object on the bottom. Use of an underwater sled will be discussed under searching techniques but construction of a sled rightly belongs here. A simple square piece of 5/8 inch marine plywood (approximately two feet square) with a hole drilled in each of the two forward corners for the towing rope and a hand hold for the diver is the most simple type of underwater sled. From there you could add handles for the diver's convenience, a T-bar for the diver's feet, and even sled to boat communications. The communication system normally consists of a button switch on the sled and a light board on the boat and can be constructed easily.

Another easily constructed rig of much use to the wreck searcher is the trawl door rig which, on a sandy bottom, can be very effective in locating remains quickly. Basically, this rig, as with the underwater sled, is towed behind your boat and with the forward motion of the boat the doors spread out until the line between them is drawn taut. This line between the doors will snag on an obstruction or, hopefully, the remains of your wreck and bring the doors together and your small boat to a halt. The fine points of using the trawl doors will be discussed under search techniques but basically all there is to the doors themselves is a wooden flat surface approximately two and one half feet square (like a planing board) with weights along one edge to make the doors stand upright on the bottom and two lines to the boat and one line between the doors. The efficiency from the trawl door rig arises from the fact that most of these rigs utilize almost one hundred feet of line between the doors which makes each leg of the grid search a fairly wide area.

A final tool which is of some use in certain situations is a grappling hook; but the efficiency of this tool is quite a bit less than the other tools mentioned. As with the sled and trawl door rigs it is towed behind your boat and will, hopefully, snag the remains of your shipwreck. The most obvious disadvantage to the use of a grapple is that the ocean is very large and the hook very small.

After you have located your wrecksite or at least a portion of it a second set of tools comes into play—those necessary to work on the wrecksite. Probably the first two or three dives on your newly found wrecksite will be the most enjoyable and important. First of all, you have to determine whether the wreck you have found is the one you were searching for and how large an area it covers. If it is a deep water wreck and fairly intact your task is considerably more simple but if it is located at a medium depth or in shallow water you will have to look for important clues. You must consider the cause of the wreck and the age of the vessel concerned. If it was a 19th century sailing vessel and wrecked due to a storm be very careful when checking out this area as there will probably be more wrecks of the same vintage in the vicinity lost due to similar conditions in what appears, at the outset, to be a bad area. If the vessel was lost due to unnatural causes (collision, pilot error, etc.) you have probably found your wreck as unnaturally caused wrecks usually occur singly rather than in groups. As you begin your search through the wreck remains you should carry certain tools with you at all times. If you can afford one, an underwater camera is of much importance to aid in your determination of how the wreck is lying (what direction) and any important clues as to the type of vessel you have found should be photographed and a record kept of their position in relation to the "center of wreckage." Every shallow water wreck seems to have a mass of remains which is almost always definable as the center of wreckage around which the rest of the remains will be found randomly. An underwater slate or underwater paper is useful in mapping the relationship of one object to another during these first dives and throughout the duration of your excavation. The use of a good underwater compass will readily aid you in this mapping task and will be important if you work out a diagrammatic of the wreck later. Exact distances can be determined using a knotted line and this should be taken along with the compass and measurements should be made using compass bearings from the center of wreckage to all major finds. To relocate particular finds when you are first studying the remains you can carry light line and a personal marker buoy (preferably an inflatable one) so that if you must surface after making an important find you will not lose its location on the returning descent because of camouflaging growth or whatever.

These few but necessary tools are extremely important on your first

dives and will save much time on successive dives. After you have made
these first few survey dives at the new wrecksite you must decide whether
or not you intend to work extensively on this wrecksite or simply choose
to recover a few artifacts and mark in your wreck log that this wreck has
been located. If you decide to stay at the site and search for some really
neat and historical artifacts more tools will come into play providing you
choose to follow the proper archaeological sequence.

An underwater grid system should be set up at least in the area of the
center of wreckage. Possibly the easiest method of doing so is through the
use of small pieces of pipe (about three feet in length) and light line. To
begin, use a short handled sledge hammer and carefully anchor four pipes
in the bottom at the extremities of the search area. Run a line around the
perimeter of the area fastening it at each corner and then using the light
line divide the square grid into smaller sections no more than ten feet
square. Photograph each square from an equal distance above the bottom
and you will be able to build a composite picture of the site for further
reference. Label each square as you photograph it for the proper sequence
of pictures in your composite. Your topside map should now be filling in
as the relationship of one object to another becomes perfectly clear. If
you can gain access to an underwater metal detector make a dive to
determine the metallic ''hot spots'' on your site and after everything has
been photographed and mapped as to its exact location you can start a
systematic search of the gridded area for artifacts using the tools to be
discussed in the next section of this chapter.

If your wreck is fairly intact—to the degree where a grid system is not
necessary—or entirely intact, such as a modern freighter or fishing
vessel might be, there are several different tools which you can utilize.
Wreck diving in an intact wreck is very much like cave diving—
you must remember that you cannot simply go straight up to the
surface if you have to. The first thing that you must understand about an
intact wreck is that even in the daytime it is dark inside. Therefore, take a
light and maybe even a spare one in case your bulb blows out or you drop
your light through a hole in the deck. A life line is a must if you intend to
go below decks to view the Captain's cabin or the engine room. A
submersible gauge on your regulator should also be a must so that you
can monitor your air supply at all times and an octopus rig (an additional
second stage on your regulator) or a pony bottle (a small tank with a
separate regulator for an emergency backup system) is something to think
about too in case you or your buddy run out of air. Another helpful hint
which might turn out to be a lifesaver is to carry with you several small
sections of good line in your goody bag for securing any doors which may

be open and swinging in the current. Again, carry your camera and photograph any items of importance to aid in identifying this wreck as your wreck but in the case of most intact or nearly intact wrecks there usually isn't much guesswork involved particularly if your pre-dive research has turned up a picture of the vessel.

If for some reason you decide to make a decompression dive or simply want to make a safety stop in the case of a fairly deep dive or one of long duration there is a good system of using your wreck as an anchor to make your safety stop accurate. If you have ever had occasion to make a safety stop on an anchor line while at sea you will know why I strongly recommend against it. A boat moving up and down in a swell will make your ten foot safety stop vary from two to fifteen feet as the boat rocks and depending on the size of the swell. This is absolutely no good at all for the diver who needs a mandatory ten foot safety stop. Carrying an expendable piece of line with you is a much better idea. Fasten this line to your wreck when you begin your ascent and when you reach the ten foot mark tie the line to your weight belt or arm while you make your stop. When you are ready to surface drop the line to the wreck and it will be there for your team on the next trip to the wreck. It works!

The final category of equipment necessary for wreck diving is that needed for the recovery of your artifacts in good condition. Artifacts come in many sizes, shapes, weights, and of many different materials. The equipment necessary to retrieve these artifacts must be equally varied. There are several personal tools which are most effective in removing objects from the bottom or from the hull of your wreck and other tools for retrieving them. A medium sized brick hammer is probably the number one choice of most divers to use in almost any situation. By its shape it has a long blade which can be used as a crowbar or screwdriver if necessary and also a hammer head with which encrustations can be removed in case you aren't sure whether that object is an artifact or a rock. Other personal tools which might be helpful on a modern wreck include a cold chisel, adjustable wrench, pliers, and a standard screwdriver.

Once your artifact is free of the bottom or the hull of the vessel you need something to put it in to return it to the surface. A diver's goody bag or a wire basket are very good for carrying small or medium sized objects. For very small or very large artifacts something else must be used, however, in order not to lose them. A large artifact should be buoyed at once and can be brought up later in the dive. For very small items such as a single coin, small coppering nails, small spikes, etc., there are two very good methods for searching and recovery.

If your project is a large one and your budget will allow it the use of an air lift or water lift is definitely the answer but involves much equipment and expense. To rig an air lift you must first have a large volume compressor on the surface. Air is pumped through a small diameter hose (approximately ¾ inch diameter) which is attached to a larger tube (approximately four to six inches in diameter) near its mouth. This tube will usually be from thirty to fifty feet in length and will lead away from the site you are working on to a dump area or to your boat on the surface. As the air from the compressor travels through the small hose and into the larger tube it will seek to return to the surface and will travel back through the larger tube creating a vacuum and resulting suctioning effect. As the mouth of the tube is moved along the bottom by divers this underwater vacuum will suck up any small particles, sand, small rocks, and any small artifacts in its path. At the discharge end of the tube there should be a sifter or a series of sifters which will allow the small artifacts to be separated from the sand and rocks.

In some sites a smaller air lift tube (one to three inches in diameter) will be desirable in order that small, fragile artifacts will not be broken by being picked up and transferred through the larger tube. In this instance a second diver would be stationed at the mouth of the air lift whose job it would be to pick out small artifacts as they are uncovered and prevent them from being damaged. All in all, the air lift is a fantastic piece of equipment which improves the efficiency of any team of wreck searchers. A variation of the air lift is the hydro lift. This unit simply uses high pressure water instead of air but with the same general end result.

For the budget concious wreck searcher there are two tricks which, although not as efficient as an air or hydro lift, can be utilized for the same general purpose. The first is a fairly new idea which works well on shallow water sites. The "thruster" is a fairly simple innovation which entails applying a directing or deflecting shield to the force produced by an outboard motor. The first and most important step involved here is to anchor your boat precisely over the spot to be cleared using four anchors (one at each corner of the boat) to insure stability over the working area. Place the thruster, which can simply be an aluminum pipe slightly larger than the diameter of the propeller, around the propeller and fasten it to the boat so it won't be washed away by the thrust of the propeller. By attaching an elbow to this pipe about six inches behind the propeller so that the force of the propeller wash will be deflected downward the rig is ready for action. Start the motor and put the engine in gear and the force of the prop wash will clear away the sand and light sediment from your working area. This method is fairly effective and definitely economical.

An even more economical but far less efficient system is to work by hand and fan away the light sediment and sand from the work site. The disadvantages to this system are that the diver's air consumption increases greatly and, even more important, that the visibility becomes much reduced from the stirred up bottom sediments. A shortcut which will sometimes make fanning the bottom by hand easier is to use a weighted ping pong paddle but more directional control is gained with the diver's own hand.

Now that you have your artifact, whether it is large, medium or small, uncovered you must transport it back to your support craft safely and efficiently. For very small items which would fall through the holes in a goody bag the easiest method for retrieval is to use a small can or plastic container with a plastic lid. Even the smallest of artifacts will not escape and the diver can even cut a small x in the top to make poking small nails and coins into it easier. These small cans should be hand carried by every member of the team for the best possible efficiency. For medium and large size objects there are two choices for getting them off the bottom and up to your boat: hauling them by hand or winch (if your boat is large enough) or lifting them through the use of compressed air. Lifting an object is probably the most common and easiest method to use. Various objects can be used to raise differently weighted artifacts. For lightweight objects a one hundred pound lift bag is ideal. It can be carried by the diver during his working time on the bottom and inflated from his exhaust bubbles or directly from his regulator. Another easy method requires inner tubes. By cutting out a small section of tube and running a line through the hollow tube you have made a twenty to thirty pound lift bag. Simple but effective! A discarded Navy sea bag lined with a plastic trash can liner also makes a fine lift bag affording the diver about two hundred pounds capacity and for really large objects such as cannon a five hundred pound lift bag or a fifty-five gallon oil drum will allow the diver to easily lift approximately five hundred pounds of artifact. With a little bit of thought there are innumerable objects which can be used to lift artifacts of almost any size to the surface.

That, in a nutshell, covers most of the equipment that you will need to buy or be able to make in order to locate, work on, and recover artifacts from most wrecksites whether in shallow or deep water. Now we must go into some detail as to how to use your locating equipment in order quickly (or at least eventually) to locate your much sought after shipwreck.

3 Search Techniques

WITHOUT question, the most difficult job for the wreck searcher is the actual task of locating the wrecksite itself. In the previous chapter the tools employed in the search were mentioned but the proper method and sequence of using these tools has been left to this chapter. The focal point of the entire search is the grid system. Properly employed the grid system will make your search effective and successful but used incorrectly it will quickly reduce your level of enthusiasm and thus your effectiveness. Before entering a discussion of techniques of searching or even the use of the grid itself the subject of seamanship and basic navigation should be explored.

It will be easily understood that you should not attempt a major wreck search until you have grasped a fundamental working knowledge of seamanship, small boat handling, and basic navigation; but most divers are not boatmen and vice versa. Possibly the best way to begin to learn these basics of boat handling is to take a course offered by the Coast Guard or local Power Squadron. These courses are usually offered to the public at no cost and provide the interested student with a wealth of basic information concerning small boats and seamanship. At the price it's well worth it, for the benefits that you will derive from it are numerous. The next step is practice and the more experience you acquire the better are the odds that you will be a successful wreck hunter. For fun, and while you are gaining experience, take your diving partner out in shallow water and tow him awhile on an underwater sled. You will both gain experience from building a sled and you will learn how best to use it on the bottom and from the boat. It is also important when your team begins actual wreck searching that more than one person on the team be able to run the boat. In fact, every member in your team should be able to perform any necessary function of the team in order that one member of the team does not become indispensible.

Searching in different depths of water requires varied techniques and a

multiplicity of different equipment. If it is possible, use electronic gear
when in deeper water rather than a diver on a sled because one of the most
valuable items that you have on your search is the air in your tanks and it
is not common for a team to carry a dozen or more tanks for a day's
search. The trawl door rig is another good deeper water technique
provided the area is not a rocky one. The United States Coast and
Geodetic Survey provides charts of every coastal area in the United States
and these charts yield a wealth of information regarding depth, bottom
types, land ranges, etc.

The day will finally arrive when you are ready to undertake your first
wreck search. Hopefully, you will have done your homework well and
have narrowed down the search area to at least one half mile square.
Assuming, for this hypothetical example, that your wreck lies about
three quarters of a mile offshore and there is a marked submerged reef
(which the vessel may have struck) about one quarter of a mile west
northwest of the proposed location of the wrecked vessel, you should
have drawn up a grid using one hundred foot squares and covering the
entire area for about one quarter of a mile on each side of the proposed
site. Your next step is to locate the center of the grid and begin your
search there. Since you wish to find the spot that is approximately one
quarter of a mile east southeast (the reciprocal of west northwest is east
southeast) of the submerged reef and is in open water, your next step is to
run a measured mile with your boat loaded the way it will be on the actual
run and under approximately the same weather and sea conditions. This
is usually most easily done by running between two buoys or a buoy and
another fixed point, whichever most closely approximates the one mile
distance. You make note that at a given speed, say 5 knots, it takes you
twelve minutes to run one nautical mile and this tells you that one quarter
mile at 5 knots is about a three minute timed run:

$$12 \text{ minutes}/1 \text{ mile} = ? \text{ minutes}/\tfrac{1}{4} \text{ mile}$$

Your third step is to make a three minute run from the marked reef on
an east southeast course and when that point is reached you should drop a
weighted buoy to mark the approximate center of your grid (which is also
your approximated position of the wreck). Be sure to check the charts
beforehand for the depth of water here so that you will not lose your
buoy by not having enough line attached to the weight. Set out three
buoys in each of two parallel lines with the grid center buoy being
centered within the first four buoys dropped. These buoys should be at
least one hundred feet apart and two hundred feet apart would not be

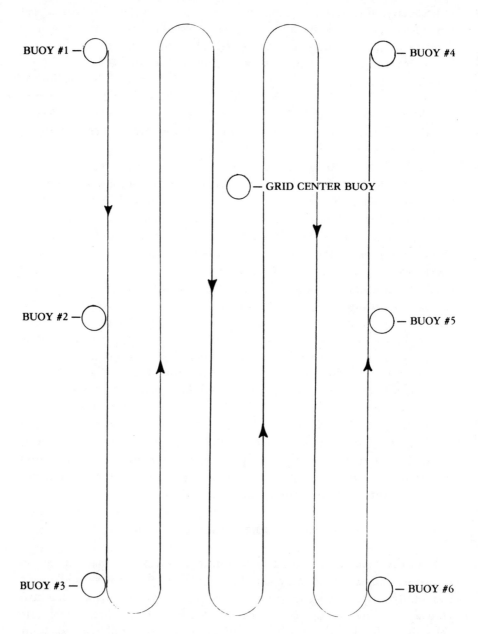

BUOY #1 —

BUOY #4

— GRID CENTER BUOY

BUOY #2 —

— BUOY #5

BUOY #3 —

— BUOY #6

Grid (First Layout)

excessive. If the water is not more than fifty or sixty feet deep and the visibility is at least ten or fifteen feet, begin sledding between the two parallel lines until the area has been thoroughly searched. (See Diagram) If that area proves negative, move the middle pair of buoys away from the grid center buoy and resume your search in this newly made square. If this area proves negative move one parallel line of buoys from the square you have marked off an equal distance but on the other side of the other parallel line leaving the grid center buoy and the original two buoys not moved at their original locations. While these areas are being eliminated as possible sites one member of the team in the boat should be crossing off on his master grid the areas already searched with negative results. In this

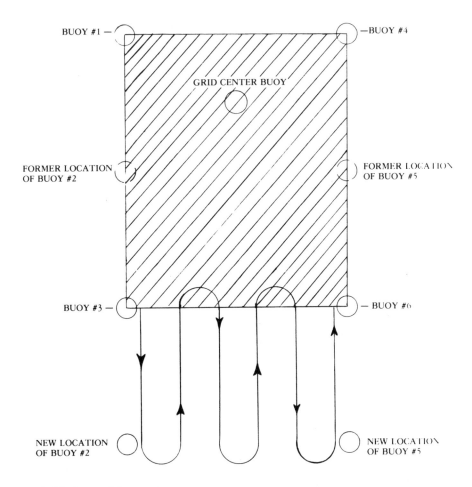

Grid (Second Layout)

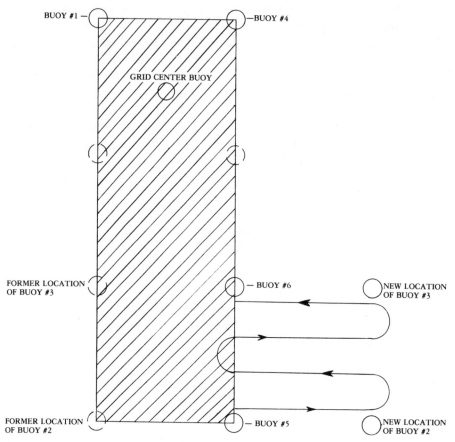

Grid (Third Layout)

way you will continue to move one line of buoys past the other until you have searched an increasingly large rectangular area in which the central grid buoy remains as the focal point.

Your search pattern on the marked off grid sheet will soon appear as a definite rectangle surrounding the first area searched and you should continue in this manner until you have covered the entire proposed site or until you have concluded that your wreck either was not in this area or has been removed.

At the end of your day's search you have the option of removing all your buoys including the grid center buoy or of leaving that focal point buoy in place. If you have not located the wreck within, say, two hundred feet on each side of the grid center buoy you are probably better off leaving it there as it will help you pick up where you left off on the next

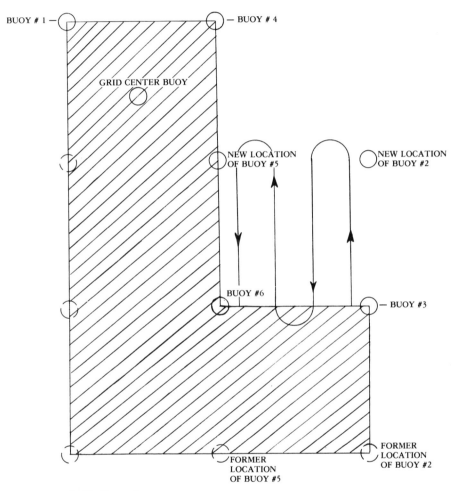

Grid (Fourth Layout)

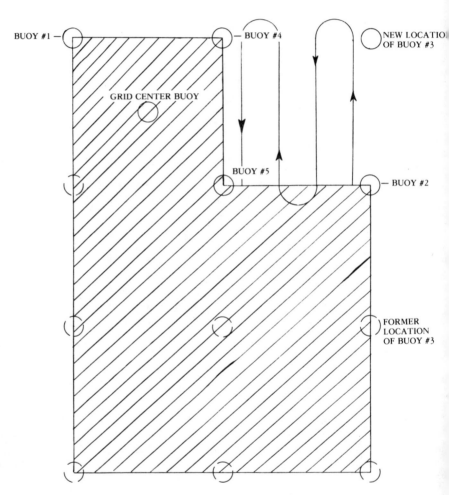

Grid (Fifth Layout)

# 8	# 7	# 6
# 9	**GRID CENTER BUOY** ◯	# 5
# 10	**LAYOUT # 1**	# 4
# 11	# 2	# 3

Grid (Layout)

trip. However, it is possible to take all your buoys and recalculate (with some margin of error) the point of the grid center buoy by making another timed run from the marked reef. Also, if you are close enough to shore to make out prominent points you may be able to take land ranges on the exact location of your grid center buoy using the following technique. A land range consists of two points on land which are of different heights and lie in a direct line. An example of a good land range is a tall building that you can see and which has lined up directly behind it a taller water tower or radio tower or even a mountain. The further apart the objects used for a range are located the more accurate the range will be. To use land ranges effectively you should have at least two different sets of ranges with an angle of at least ninety degrees between them from where you are viewing them. The accuracy of this type of ranges is almost pinpoint. One set of ranges to a local wreck in Rhode Island will put divers within twenty feet of the center of wreckage of that vessel every time. Use caution when taking ranges, however, and never use a moveable object such as a buoy (which may be pulled off its normal position by a storm) in your set of range points.

Using the grid pattern discussed the next topic is a detailed study of the use of the underwater sled, trawl door rig, circle searching and other techniques of searching your gridded area in quest of the elusive shipwreck.

The underwater sled, as I mentioned before, is probably the most important tool that the small-scale wreck searcher has at his disposal. It is easy to build, easy to use, high on efficiency and makes the job of searching the bottom for a ship's bones a fun dive as well as a working dive. We have discussed the construction; the operation we will undertake to discuss here. It takes only a two man team to begin a sledding operation—a boat operator and a diver. When the team has reached the site and set out the necessary buoys the boat operator can rig the sled while the diver dresses. To rig the sled to the boat requires attaching a rope bridle to the boat so the towline will take an even strain on the transom, and fastening the line from the bridle to the sled itself. This becomes slightly more complicated if the sled is provided with communications to the boat. In this case, the wiring for the button on the sled must be attached to the battery and light board on the boat. Signalling with this type of system will vary but is usually similar to the following: one flash—OK or GO; two flashes—slow down; three flashes—speed it up; and four flashes—STOP (I am dropping off the sled to investigate something). If you are using a sled without communications it is standard practice to attach a buoy with plenty of line to the towed diver and have a member of the team watch for the buoy to stop as the sledding operation is in progress. This will indicate that the diver has dropped off the sled and is investigating something. The importance of this is that without this marker buoy you can conceivably continue to tow the empty sled because the pressure of the water against the moving sled will make it appear as if the diver is still on the sled. When the diver is ready to begin he will enter the water, submerge (clearing his ears) and when on the bottom and ready to go he will give two or three tugs on the towline to indicate that he is ready to begin the operation. There is one important limitation to the use of an underwater sled—bad visibility. The diver must have enough visibility to see what is coming toward him or he may collide with rocks or maybe even with the sought after wreck. Usually ten or fifteen feet of visibility is a necessary minimum. One final note concerning the use of a sled or for that matter any towed device—you must use enough line to

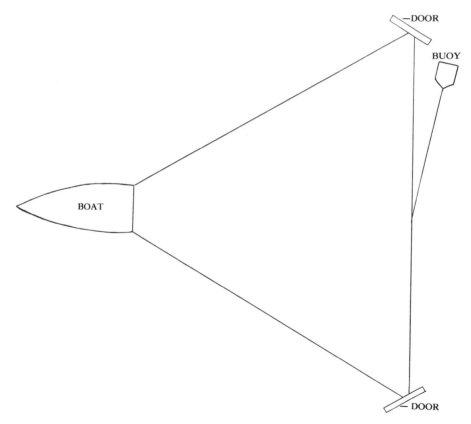

Trawl Door Rig

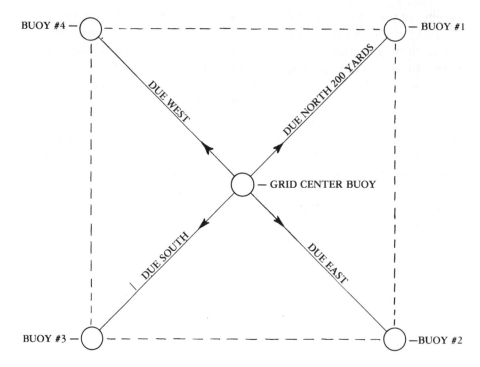

Trawl Door Rig (Towing Pattern)

enable the object to stay on the bottom. Usually three times the depth is the rule of thumb for the length of line necessary to tow a sledding diver but even a little more than that is not too much. Be careful also of your towing speed or you may have a very irate teammate on your hands. About two to four knots should be maximum speed and slightly slower isn't too bad either!

The trawl door rig is probably the most convenient tool to use in sandy areas and more than once has proven to be very efficient. Although similar in use to the underwater sled the technique is somewhat different. Attaching the doors to the boat requires two lines, one to each door, and between the doors there is another small line about six inches from the bottom. It is usually a good idea to tie off a buoy to the middle of this line between the doors as it will rise to the surface as the doors come together indicating that you have snagged either your wreck or an obstruction. If we were using this rig in the example mentioned the best buoy layout to set up is quite different from that mentioned for sledding.

Once again you would locate the position for and drop the grid center buoy. This will be the focal point of the search but before you set up the trawl door rig and begin your search you should drop four buoys as follows. Your first run should follow a major compass point for a distance of up to two hundred yards from the grid center buoy at which point a buoy should be dropped. Return to the grid center buoy and start your second run on another major compass point. After running about the same distance your second buoy should be dropped and again you can return to the grid center buoy and start your third run on still another major compass point. After four basic runs you will have set up a square pattern with the four buoys you have dropped covering an area roughly two hundred and eighty yards square. (See Diagram) This will be your

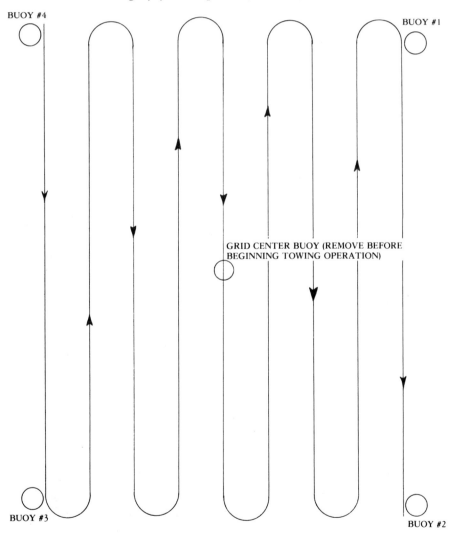

BUOY #4

BUOY #1

GRID CENTER BUOY (REMOVE BEFORE BEGINNING TOWING OPERATION)

BUOY #3

BUOY #2

first major search area. Note: Before you set out the trawl rig you should remove the grid center buoy (taking ranges on its location if you can) so that your trawl rig will not be caught on it.

Begin your search at one corner of the square and by running about nine overlapping parallel legs you will have covered the area within that basic square. Mark off the area you have covered on your master grid and repeat the search procedure in an adjacent square leaving the original grid square buoys in position (as was done in the sledding search). Following this pattern all the way around the original grid square will require nine buoy set ups in total, and you will have searched an area approximately eight hundred yards (or approximately one half mile) square.

This system obviously is effective in covering a large amount of area but there are several disadvantages which must be mentioned. First, and most important, whenever the trawl rig catches an obstruction it must be checked out by a diver to see whether it is your desired wreck or simply a rock which shouldn't be lying in this sandy area. Secondly, a problem which sometimes accompanies the use of a trawl door rig is that it may pick up seaweed and other growth on the bottom and when a sufficient weight of weed is caught it will begin to pull the doors together as if you were hung up on an obstruction. Obviously, both disadvantages of this system center on the fact that the rig has no eyes and requires that a diver be ready to check it out each and every time it gets hung up or appears so.

A third technique of searching which can be used when searching either from a boat or from shore is the circle search. This requires only one buoy and two lengths of line per diver and particularly in rocky areas where the visibility is poor it has proven to be effective in many instances. Again, to begin the search you must locate the grid center which is as near as possible to your wreck. Starting from this point use one length of line to anchor your buoy and tie the other line (of approximately one hundred foot length) to the buoy line about three feet above the bottom. Swim to the end of your tether line on a fixed compass point and from this point, with your tether line taut, begin to swim a circle around the anchored buoy. If there are any obstructions between you and the buoy your line will catch on them and bring you to them in an ever decreasing circle. If there are no obstructions (or your wreck) within the circle you will return to the spot where you began your circle. By anchoring your tether line at this spot you can follow the line back to the anchored buoy and move this buoy to the spot where the tether line is tied.

After marking off the area that you have searched on your underwater slate, repeat the circle search going one hundred feet further from the spot where you started the first circle and begin circling again. This second

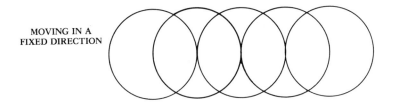

MOVING IN A
FIXED DIRECTION

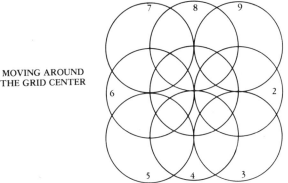

MOVING AROUND
THE GRID CENTER

FROM	TO	MOVE
1	2	NORTH
2	3	EAST
3	4	SOUTH
4	5	SOUTH
5	6	WEST
6	7	WEST
7	8	NORTH
8	9	NORTH

Circle Search Techniques

circle will overlap the first which makes your chance of error in that circle even less. After you have completed your second circle and noted this on your master grid you have the option of continuing in the same direction which will make your search proceed in a straight line or you can take a different compass point (which should be adjacent to the point that you have already used) and in this way move around the grid center in one hundred foot circles. (See Diagram) As long as you continue to mark off the areas as you search them you will not have to worry about duplicating a previous circle. Although this technique is not as efficient as sledding or using the trawl rig, in some situations this is the most efficient means at hand.

There are two other searching techniques which are used but we will touch on these only briefly as there efficiency is questionable. The first of these final techniques is grappling. This involves simply dragging a grappling hook or perhaps even an anchor across the bottom behind a boat in hopes of hooking into the wrecked remains. Like the trawl door rig a grapple lacks the benefit of eyes; unlike that rig a grappling hook covers an extremely small area in width. Even if a series of hooks on a bar is used the total width of your search per leg will not be more than five or six feet at the most. The only favorable thing to be said for a grappling system is that it goes where the boat operator desires. For relocating a wreck when you have only limited land ranges a grapple can be of assistance to the wreck searcher but in general this system is a last resort. The second of these ineffective searching techniques is probably the least effective system to be used, namely, the free swimming technique. It is most often used in diving from shore by an inexperienced wreck searcher and involves only an equipped diver possibly towing a buoy at best. If the particular free swimming diver is adept in the use of an underwater compass the efficiency of this search technique is slightly improved but in general there is little to be said in favor of swimming around at random in search of your shipwreck. On the positive side, however, if the diver is adept in the use of an underwater compass there will be situations where all other means are of little or no use to the searcher—such as an area with extremely large boulders and very good visibility in shallow water. The use of a sled here is dangerous, a trawl door rig is ridiculous, a circle search ineffective, and a grappling hook useless. In this situation the free swimming technique is just about the only one with any effectiveness at all.

One word concerning searching techniques when using electronic equipment. As with all your searches try to locate and mark the grid center first. With electronics you can cover a larger area of bottom more rapidly so your second step is to lay out your buoys for your square grid in a manner similar to that used when you employ the trawl door rig. You may decide to set your buoys at a slightly longer distance from the grid center buoy for this type of search, but it probably will not be desirable to try to search too large an area at first. And remember: you want to be able to keep your buoys in sight to make each run as efficient as possible. I would recommend that your square not exceed three hundred and fifty square yards in area and as you place buoys further away from each other and the grid center buoy you should make them taller for better visibility (i.e. the use of a buoy with a flag above the water two or three feet at least).

These techniques when used efficiently and properly should make your searching much more effective and more often successful than if used improperly or ignored. There are a few search techniques that you might employ at your wrecksite after you have located it that should be mentioned. Needless to say, these techniques relate to a wreck which has been scattered or broken up to some degree and would not be necessary on an intact or nearly intact wreck. When a site has been located the first searching dive should utilize a derivation of the circle search technique. Using a buoy and anchor system and a short tether rope of no more than twenty five foot length, search the area around the starting point for more wreckage. If more wreckage is found move your buoy to it and continue until more wreckage is not to be found. When you run out of wreckage leave a buoy to mark the outer limit of the wreckage in that direction and return to your starting point to make another run to determine how far the wreckage lies in another direction.

After you have made about eight trips you should have the extremities of the wreck pretty well marked off and you can begin to search within these limits for the hot spots that you may desire to dig into later. After these hot spots are located and marked on your grid of the wrecksite you must decide whether you want to search into them further or simply to make a superficial search and then look for another wreck. If you decide to stay you should set up a rope grid as explained in an earlier chapter, photograph the areas within this grid and then employ one of the several tools mentioned for finding and retrieving artifacts.

One final word must be mentioned with regard to your physical search for the wreck itself. Never approach your day of wreck searching with only one plan in mind. Weather and sea conditions play a large role in every search and you should have an alternate wreck site planned so that if you cannot go to your number one site because of these conditions or if you have spent four or five hours unsuccessfully searching for your wreck at the site you will have an alternative site at which to make a dive (preferably on a wreck you have previously located and would like to visit again). This is of great importance particularly in regard to your team's morale and enthusiasm. There is nothing that will kill a potential wreck diver's enthusiasm more quickly than spending a month of weekends in an unsuccessful search for a wreck and nothing that will pique their enthusiasm more than to locate a difficult one which has been eluding them for several dives. Wreck searching is not an easy task but it is an extremely rewarding one.

The final step in your wreck search and recovery is the removal and preservation of artifacts which is the next and last subject of methodology which we shall explore.

4 Artifacts: Recovery and Preservation

WRECK diving has many appealing features to offer the diver including super spearfishing, lobstering, and exploring, but two in particular stand out as the prime reasons for hunting wrecks: underwater photography and artifact retrieval. As the amount of shipwreck legislation increases (for the protection of historical underwater sites) the interest in underwater photography increases proportionally but the thrill of recovering a ship's bell or wheel always stays in my mind as the most pleasurable of these two aspects of wreck diving.

Step one was to research the vessel's history and the story of its demise; step two was to physically locate the remains of the vessel; and step three is to locate, recover and preserve the pieces of history from the much sought-after shipwreck. Artifacts come in many shapes, sizes and of many different materials and usually each wreck diver has a specific type of artifact in mind. It is a wise diver, indeed, who seeks only to recover one nice artifact from each wreck he searches for (unless he is searching for wrecks of particular historical importance). This gives him something rewarding to remember the search by and does not place him in the category of a junkman who seeks only the monetary gains from the sale of scrap metal. Also, this leaves to future wreck divers the possibility of locating this wreck and recovering their own artifacts.

As mentioned in the previous chapter, the wreck diver should begin his artifact search by marking off the extremities of the remains. By noting on an underwater slate or treated paper the more important finds the diving team can usually reconstruct the vessel on paper so that they can determine in which direction the vessel lies, how it is listing (either to port or starboard), and where the key areas to search for specific artifacts are. When actually searching a specific area the diver should always carry: an underwater slate, a lift bag, at least one inflatable marker buoy, and a length of line to attach to the buoy. Tools for removing a difficult artifact from its location can be left on the support vessel or, if diving from shore, can be towed on an inner tube or some other flotation device. Once the sought after artifact has been located the diver can buoy it and return to the boat for any tools needed to extricate it from its position. Before discussing further the removal process a word of caution should be mentioned concerning the possible dangers to be encountered with certain types of wrecks and wreckage.

If the shipwreck sought was a wooden vessel and lies in fairly shallow water in pieces it is generally a safe wreck and has few hazardous "diver traps". A "diver trap" is simply a situation which may be potentially dangerous to the searcher in terms of being something that could fall on him, trap him inside, or in some other way impede his free swimming motion. When searching in the remains of a broken-up, metal-hulled wreck the diver must be wary of sharp metal edges that can severly cut him (even through a thick wet suit) and he should be careful to avoid swimming under large plates from the hull as they might fall at any time. These two situations are even more dangerous if there is a strong current in the area of the wreck and the cautious diver will definitely be the safest diver.

An intact wreck presents even more diver traps than the other types of wrecks mentioned. Besides the sharp metal edges to cut the diver and the large metal objects to fall on him there are doors and hatches to close on the diver possibly locking him inside. An ambitious artifact searcher will almost always first seek out the engine room which, being located at the lowest level of the ship, will mean a trip through companionways and probably through several hatches. A little time taken to tie back each door or hatch or even to prop metal objects against them to prevent their accidental closing will be well invested. A safety line is a must if a deep penetration of the vessel is desired because, as in cave diving, you can't simply go straight up to the surface if you want to and you must be able to retrace your route to the outside.

Many wreck divers will not penetrate an intact wreck without a pony bottle. Basically, a pony bottle system is simply the use of an additional small tank with its own regulator as a back up system in case of regulator malfunction or in case the diver runs out of air because he failed to use a submersible pressure gauge (which would monitor his tank pressure at all times) or even worse, he ignored that gauge, relying on his reserve air to be enough to bring him back to the surface. Don't be fooled—when you are enthralled with the sights that a large wreck will offer, your air will be consumed all too quickly!

The recovery of artifacts will utilize the tools already mentioned with the easiest lifting aid being the air in your tank. A lift bag, large barrel, a navy sea bag lined with a trash bag, or an inner tube were all mentioned as fine tools for lifting almost any size artifact to the surface. If your wreck is in the open this task will be fairly simple but if you are inside an intact wreck the task can be much more complex. In this situation you must first make sure that your artifact is completely free of any encumbrances and then move it to the nearest exit for a direct route to the surface. Often, if your artifact is medium sized, you can utilize your lift bag to relieve the object of its weight, short of making it buoyant, and then pull it by hand to the exit—at which point you can add more air to the lift bag and send it to the surface. If the object is very large you can again relieve it of some of its weight and use a come-along to pull it to the nearest exit. This type of operation may require several dives and you should be careful to pace yourself in this task so as not to exhaust yourself (and your air supply) in attempting to remove the artifact on one dive. Also, if your support vessel is large enough you can haul aboard your artifact or even a basket of small artifacts collected by all the divers. Small artifacts such as coins, deck spikes, coppering nails, etc., can be collected by using an air lift or hydro lift as described before or, if they are readily observable, they can be placed in a recovery bag or small can to be hand carried back to the surface.

Once you have your artifact or artifacts aboard your support vessel and the diving for the day has been terminated your task of preserving the artifacts begins—immediately! If your artifact is of a ferrous nature (iron or steel) or wood it should be kept in a salt water or fresh water bath during the trip home to slow down the oxidation rate which will start to destroy the ferrous material as soon as it is exposed to the air. If your artifact is of a non-ferrous material (such as brass, bronze or copper) the water bath is not necessary as these metals do not break down chemically in the same manner as the ferrous metals. Silver and gold artifacts will also be preservable with little or no treatment. Silver in salt water will oxidize unless it is in the close proximity of a ferrous metal of higher valence. If this is the case the silver will be afforded a "cathodic protection" and the other metal will receive the damage from the salts in the water while the silver will remain almost untouched. If there is no metal nearby to afford this protection the silver will eventually completely disappear leaving only a black powder (silver oxide). Gold will normally remain perfectly preserved with little or no damage other than the possibility of some calcareous growth. Porcelain and glassware artifacts generally will survive the corrosive action of seawater with but few harmful results. To transport them to the shore you should take care when handling them so that they will not be broken. A water bath for these artifacts is not necessary.

Once on shore the preservation process of each different type of artifact should be undertaken. With the exception of ferrous metals I have found the preservation of artifacts to be a not too difficult task. The non-ferrous metals, porcelain and glass objects will usually have a layer of calcareous growth on them which is simply barnacles, limpet shells, coral, etc. and the removal of these deposits is a fairly simple task. The use of brick acid (a solution of muriatic acid available in most hardware stores) is most common and very effective in removing this calcareous growth. Normally this solution is approximately twenty per cent strength and I have found that it is best to dilute this solution to about half normal strength or about a ten per cent solution. This solution can be kept in a plastic or glass container and the artifact placed within, or the solution can be painted on the artifact with a small brush. The solution will bubble as it eats away the calcareous growth and when the bubbling stops the artifact can be rinsed in fresh water and scrubbed lightly to remove all of the growth. When using this or any acidic solution use rubber gloves and avoid all contact with your skin and you will find that it is a safe and effective way to restore your artifact to its original condition. The brass or copper artifact must then be polished and mounted and you will have a finished artifact of gleaming beauty. With glass or porcelain artifacts there is a little more cleaning involved and the use of household ammonia or lye will remove all but the toughest stains. For wooden artifacts such as a deadeye or a wooden block there are different processes that can be used. The complex process involves the use of a solution of hot alum into which the wooden object is placed and left until the solution has saturated the wood. This process is based on the principal that the alum will replace the water in the wooden object and thus support the wood and preserve it. An easier process that I have found to be adequate is to allow the wooden artifact to dry out completely for a period of two or three weeks and then to fill the pores completely with sometimes as many as ten coats of varnish. Using this method wooden artifacts up to about one hundred and sixty years old have been preserved.

Without doubt, the most difficult type of artifact to preserve is ferrous metal. Not only is the process difficult and time consuming, it is also very expensive and entirely necessary for these artifacts. To begin with, an iron object must not be allowed to lie in the open air because of the oxidation problem mentioned earlier and it must be reimmersed almost as soon as it has been taken from the water. The calcareous growth must be gently chipped from the object and following this the object must be placed in a solution of at least ten per cent sodium hydroxide for a period of about six weeks. If the artifact is small, like a cannon ball, this is not a difficult or expensive job but if the object is large, like the cannon itself, you will need a very large vat and many gallons of chemical.

After the first solution has done its job and the vat has been drained, "mossy" zinc must be placed around the object and a second solution of sodium hydroxide must be placed in the vat. If you have a vat set up for easy drainage and ease of handling the process is not too difficult, but if you aren't set up very efficiently there is a lot of work involved. The second solution will remain in the vat for about four weeks and at the end of this period the vat must again be drained and the zinc oxide powder that is now on the object being treated must be washed off with a mild solution of sulphuric acid. Next, the object must be washed at least three times, for about a week each time—and then the fun begins. The object must be thoroughly dried, preferably in an oven, and then coated with either a plastic solution or a clear lacquer. This really is a necessary complex process and if it is being done on a non-professional basis it will soon convince the artifact hunter that he should have stuck to picking up non-ferrous artifacts.

The final step for any artifact is its proper display. With all the time, effort and money put into recovering it, the artifacts from your wreck must be displayed to serve as a remembrance of your successful search. For brass and copper artifacts a wooden stand is probably the nicest display and mounted on a panelled wall there is nothing nicer than a porthole or a ship's bell. However, many artifacts also make exquisite objects of some usefulness—such as a steam gauge housing that has been turned into a clock housing or a porthole frame which now serves as a mirror frame or a picture frame. The possibilities are limited only by the imagination of the diver.

PART II

PREFACE

In Part I we discussed a complete methodology of searching for shipwrecks through research, tools, searching methods and the recovery and preservation of artifacts. In Part II we will see how this methodology actually works in practice. I have chosen four of the many wrecks which our divers have visited as examples of almost any situation you may encounter.

The first, the sailing ship *Lydia Skolfield* is a shallow water wooden wreck of late 19th century vintage; the second, the Spanish brig *Minerva* is another shallow water wooden sailing vessel wreck, but of early 19th century vintage and one which posed some interesting artifact recovery problems; the third, the steel tanker *Llewellyn Howland* is a 20th century vessel in somewhat deeper water which posed interesting problems in mapping the site; and the fourth, the steel fishing vessel *Hilda Garston* is a 20th century deep water wreck which is completely intact.

5 Lydia Skolfield

IT was winter again and we were hard at work in the local historical
society compiling a list of vessels which had been lost in New England
waters in preparation for the following summer. It was not unusual for us
to spend much of our free time out of the water during the frigid months
of December through April when the water temperature in southern
New England averages thirty five to forty five degrees. Wreck diving was
a fairly new aspect of our sport to us and we had been doing considerable
research into all its facets. Very few divers we knew would go to the
trouble of digging through piles of old records in search of references to
old vessels which had left their bones in our waters but, if we had nothing
else, we had enthusiasm.

As often as possible, we made arrangements to meet with knowledgeable people concerned with the early shippers and shipping in our area
and/or with wreck diving experience. At one such meeting we were
teased by a friend with the idea that there might be a wreck in the area of a
local diving spot known as Butterball Rock. Just the mention of such a
possibility was enough—we made plans immediately for a dive in this
area as soon as possible. Our first dive here proved to be almost a total
failure in terms of locating any wreck and we decided there and then to
formulate a plan of action and through research, rather than blunder, to
determine whether there actually was a wreck in this area and, if so, to
identify it and recover an artifact to show our wreck diver friend that we
knew what we were doing.

Our known facts were few: the location (if accurate or not we did not
know at the time) and the date of the disaster within about one hundred
years (the inference from our friend was that the vessel was a sailing vessel
indicative probably that it was of 19th century vintage). It seemed logical
that the vessel was fairly large as the wreck of a small vessel (50 to 100
tons) would be quickly forgotten. After several nights of searching
through the data which we had been accumulating we were able to come

up with a good possibility based on three separate references. Our first reference was the book *Storms and Shipwrecks of New England* by E. R. Snow which gave us the following information: Ship *Lydia Skolfield*—1891—Newport. The key to the map of the U.S. Army Corps of Engineers provided a second reference with a little more information as follows: Ship *Lydia Scholfield*—Rugget Point, Newport—4/19/1891—wrecked. Finally, looking into the records of the U.S. Life Saving Service for the Third Life Saving District, we confirmed our other references with the following information: April 19, 1891—Ship *Lydia Skolfield*—Ragged Point, Newport—cause: fog—condition: wrecked.

Our next move was to search through the newspaper accounts for April, 1891 and determine what we could as to the disaster, i.e., why it occurred; exactly where, if possible; and what happened to the ship after the disaster occurred (was it salvaged, did it break up and sink, could it have been pulled off the rocks?). By using the records from the most local newspaper, the Newport Daily News, we accumulated the following accounts of the disaster and the salvage efforts. The accounts are presented in their entirety so that you might have the opportunity to see just how the writers of yesterday's news chose to present their stories to the public. A few portions have been deleted, however, because of their repetitious nature.

Newport Daily News: April 20, 1891

ON THE WASH BOWL
Ship Lydia Skolfield Ashore Near Castle Hill

Ship Lydia Skolfield, Captain Masson, nineteen days from New Orleans for Providence, struck on the "Wash Bowl," or what is put down on the coast survey chart as Butler Bull Rock, just off Ocean Avenue, near Castle Hill, Sunday morning at about half-past ten o'clock, and was soon hard and fast. She was discovered by a patrolman of the life saving station at Price's Neck, and a boat's crew went to her assistance and took off the ship's crew and their personal effects. The captain's wife was also on board. A dense fog prevailed, and the captain lost his bearings. About the time the ship got comfortably settled on the rocks the fog lifted. The captain has been detained between Shinnecock Light, Montauk Point and Block Island four days on account of the fog. At 7 o'clock Saturday night Block Island was passed, and between 8 and 9 o'clock an electrical storm came up, necessitating the shortening of sail and tacking out to sea. At 4 o'clock Sunday morning it was decided to make for Newport, and three hours later the fog again shut down thick, but by throwing the lead the captain was in hopes to get through the channel all right. A sharp lookout was kept but it was impossible to see on account of the fog. The mate was on the lookout forward and when he saw the breakers to the port side supposed he was near the Dumplings across the channel, and the rudder was put to starboard; the bow cleared the rocks, but the stern struck hard. After striking the ship raised ahead and was thrown further inshore. When she struck her rudder was driven through the deck. The ship did not leak for some time after she struck, but has now five feet of water in the hold. Captain Masson contracted at once with Captain Waters, who secured lighters and today began taking out the cargo.

The stranded ship has 7,000 barrels of cotton seed oil on board, 3,500 of which are for Providence and the balance for New York. The cargo is a valuable one, each barrel being worth $32.00. There is an insurance on the cargo but the ship is not favored in that line. She is thirty-one years old and some time ago the sum of $10,000 was expended in improving her. She is a fine-looking craft and is attracting a good deal of attention from the sight-seers on Ocean Avenue. She is of 1,200 tons burden and belongs in New York.

Through the courtesy of Mr. George Pierce the crew of eleven were furnished with free passage to New York last night on steamer Plymouth. The captain and the mate, Albert Wallace, remained here.

Early this morning Captain Waters proceeded to the scene, with Tug Aquidneck and schooners J. M. Baylies, Freemont, and Young America, and at once began work getting out the cargo. Schooner Baylies was laid alongside, but her topmasts, striking the yards of the ship, interfered somewhat with the work and Captain Waters sent to Fall River for a steam lighter, which will greatly facilitate the work of unloading. The 3,500 barrels of oil for Providence are mostly between decks, and this space will first be cleared, as the men can easily work there. An attempt will be made to pump her out and float her. It is hoped that nearly one thousand barrels will be gotten out today.

A gang of about eighty-five men is employed lightering the ship, the barrels being hoisted out by steam. The ship has a strong list to starboard, is well filled with water and looks somewhat as if her back is broken, though such is not thought to be the case; both Captain Masson and Captain Waters are confident that, unless a storm sets in, the vessel and cargo will be saved, as no expense will be spared to do the work at once, before the present favorable weather changes.

Newport Daily News: April 21, 1891

The Stranded Ship

Yesterday Captain Waters succeeded in getting something over two hundred barrels of oil of ship Lydia Skolfield, ashore at Castle Hill, the work not running as smoothly as expected. These were all placed on schooner J. M. Baylies, which will take them to Providence. This morning the steam lighter arrived from Fall River and it is thought lifted out nearly five hundred barrels from between decks, the men having gotten everything into working order. Steamer R. J. Merritt of the Merritt Wrecking Company arrived this morning from Staten Island, bringing a gang of about thirty-five workers, who are engaged in stripping the rigging, taking down the yards, etc. The condition of the ship remains about the same, though the sea has freshened up considerably under the southwest wind and is making the work of unloading considerably different from what it would be at the dock.

Newport Daily News: April 22, 1891

The Stranded Ship

Work on the stranded ship Lydia Skolfield was continued yesterday afternoon and this morning under not as favorable as heretofore. The southwest wind prevailing yesterday freshened considerably in the afternoon, making a very pretty swell in the channel, and causing the white caps to dance about very lively. The lighter of the Reynold's Line, known as Harbor Transportation No. 1, was taken out to assist in unloading while the Fall River lighter was discharging in the inner harbor. Now Harbor Transportation No. 1, as its name implies, was built for harbor work and not for open sea wrecking and when towed out into the heavy sea prevailing yesterday was evidently unable to stand the strain, for, when about forty barrels of oil had been lifted onto her deck, it was found she was sinking, and the oil was at once hoisted back into the ship. Before all had been gotten back the lighter had settled by the stern, throwing the oil against the small house about the hoisting engine and completely wrecking it. The lighter was brought into the harbor this morning. She will need to go on the marine railway and have a new house built before she is ready for further work. This morning the sea was still rougher, and the wind stronger and after taking out a fair load the lighter was obliged to come in. Steam lighter Howard arrived from Providence this morning, and will, doubtless, be engaged for unloading, as schooner Cynthia Jane of Taunton has been. Yesterday the Merritt Wrecking Company took off most of the sails and some of the yards of the vessel, and today, the ship rolling so much because of the heavy top hamper all the masts were cut away, and they will be towed in this afternoon. This action greatly eased the ship, and will make the work of unloading easier.

During the work this morning Captain Waters was struck by a cask of oil, knocked down and stunned temporarily, though he escaped serious injury by the prompt action of some of the men who were nearby.

Newport Daily News: April 23, 1891

At The Wreck

Owing to the heavy sea offside, no work was done today on unloading the stranded ship, but both Captain Waters, with Tug Aquidneck and the Young America, and the Merritt Company, with their steamer and schooner, were busy saving furniture and supplies, the Merritt Company getting off the anchors, chains, etc. An empty barge has reported here for the Merritt Company and, with the change of wind to the northward, which is expected to follow this afternoon's squall, the work of saving the cargo will be pushed rapidly. Schooner J. M. Baylies has sailed for Providence with 632 barrels oil, the balance of what was saved being on schooner Emma.

Newport Daily News: April 24, 1891

The north wind made the vicinity of the wrecked ship comparatively calm today, and the wreckers are busily at work getting out the cargo. Steam lighters Archer and Howard, two schooners, a barge and Tugs Aquidneck and Merritt make the vicinity of the wreck a very lively one. It is expected that a large quantity of oil will be save, as both steam lighters have been working steadily all day.

The Providence Journal says, regarding the cargo of the stranded ship Lydia Skolfield: "The cargo of 7,000 barrels is worth $20 per barrel aboard the ship, and $32 discharged in this city. This will make the value of the cargo delivered $224,000. It is estimated that it is costing the wreckers $10 or more per barrel to remove oil, which adds $70,000 to the value of the oil. The insurance company is doing all in its power to save the wealth."

Newport Daily News: April 25, 1891

The good weather and smooth sea enabled the wreckers to save about eight hundred barrels of oil from the stranded ship yesterday, and today, the conditions remaining favorable, a very large quantity will probably be secured. All the wrecking vessels are on the scene, and the work is being rapidly pushed, as the barrels are breaking in the hold and must be saved at once, if at all.

Newport Daily News: April 27, 1891

About five hundred barrels of oil were saved from the wreck yesterday, making upwards of twenty-five hundred all told, already secured. During the day many pedestrians and owners of horses visited Castle Hill to look at the stranded ship, and not a few catboats went out and around it, the weather being very pleasant, the wind being favorable and the sea nearly as smooth as a mill pond.

Newport Daily News: April 28, 1891

Yesterday the work of the wreckers on ship Lydia Skolfield was somewhat interfered with by the wind, which, coming from the southwest in the afternoon, kicked up considerable sea. The work of unloading the between decks was continued, and some of the casks from the hold were brought up. In all about two hundred were brought out and taken in, the wreckers quitting work quite early. This morning steamer R. J. Merritt went to Providence, taking barge Chester Griswold and schooner Anthony Burton, both loaded with barrels. The number so far secured is between twenty-six and twenty-seven hundred barrels, of which Captain Waters secured between eighteen and nineteen hundred. Today steam lighters Archer and Bay View are at work.

Newport Daily News: April 29, 1891

A Visit To The Lydia Skolfield

A visit to the stranded ship Lydia Skolfield, at Castle Hill, is a very interesting event for anyone not acquainted with the method of saving cargoes from wrecks. The ship lies just to the south of Ragged Point, is headed ashore, and has a strong list to starboard; almost directly astern is the rock known as the Wash Bowl, which shows at low water, causing the spectator to wonder how a ship of the size of the Skolfield could reach her present position. The vessel evidently rests on a single rock, which has struck the after part, and probably broken the ship's back, as the rail on the after part of the starboard side is thrown out of true, as if the whole frame was broken. On board the vessel everything is activity and oil. The main and after hatchways are open and from each a steam lighter is hoisting barrels of oil as fast as possible, which, just at present, is not as fast as heretofore. Down below, in what is known as between decks, are four divers, in their rubber suits, but without their helmets, floundering around in oil, and fishing out barrels which others, not in diving uniform, but still protected by oilskin clothing, are guiding out of the hatchway. The water inside the ship comes up close to the deck, but the spectator would never imagine it to be water, for the entire surface is coated with a heavy, dark, creamy-looking mass that adheres to everything. This is the oil from fully a thousand broken barrels, which has been thickened by the cold, and covers the water to depth of several feet, and makes working on the ship a slippery and not at all pleasant job. Each barrel, as it is hoisted out, is covered at least half an inch in thickness with this thick oil, which is swept off when the barrel reaches the lighter, and can then be washed overboard or shoveled up into casks. Probably several pails of oil are lost with each barrel fished out, but there seems to be no feasible way of preventing this loss, as time is money in the wrecking business. The work of hoisting out the barrels, which is done by steam gear, is not at all like similar work at the dock. The deck pitches at quite a sharp angle, and is covered with a coating of oil that makes it as slippery as ice; the men maintain an upright position by means of cleats nailed to the deck or by hanging to ropes, and very often maintain no footing at all, bringing up against the bulwark, or pitching headlong into the oily mess in the hold. The handling of the oil-covered barrels, even in a sling, is by no means an easy task, as each cask weighs from four hundred and thirty to four hundred and eighty pounds, nearly a quarter of a ton, and, when swinging above the deck in the sling, are extremely dangerous for passers-by, as Captain Waters learned, a dent fully an inch deep in a deckhouse showing where a barrel that knocked him down afterward struck.

Work was begun on the wreck Monday, the water being quiet until Tuesday afternoon, when it came up rough, and Harbor Transportation was wrecked. Wednesday the sea was so heavy that the masts had to be cut away, and Thursday no work could be done in unloading, the sea being too rough for the lighters to lie alongside. Friday, Saturday, and Sunday with the wind from the north the sea was smooth, and good progress was made, about two thousand barrels being taken out in these three days. Yesterday the between decks having been cleared out the work was slow, as the barrels had to be fished from the hold, through the hatchways. Today the lower deck is being cut away by the divers; this will let the barrels which float come to the surface, and greatly facilitate the work of unloading.

The pounding of the ship Wednesday and Thursday broke the cargo, and the barrels rolling about in the holds were badly broken up. In some cases the hoops were knocked off, and the barrels fell to pieces; in others the strong staves were broken and the barrels are fished out, partially filled with thick oil, some of which is saved.

During the week tug Aquidneck, schooners Young America, Emma, J. M. Baylies, Anthony and Burton, steam lighters Archer, Howard and Bay View, Harbor Transportation No. 1, barges Chester Griswold and Archer and wrecking steamer R. J. Merritt have been engaged in the work, which has been under direction of Captain John Waters, with whose work Captain Masson and the mate of the ship, who remain here, and one of the owners, who came on from New York, are more than satisfied.

Captain Waters has arranged to bring a steamer with oil tanks to the vessel and pump out the oil floating inside the wreck, as in this way a considerable quantity can be saved, none having yet escaped from the vessel, though much has been washed from the wrecking vessels.

In addition to the cargo of 7,000 barrels of cotton-seed oil the vessel had on board upwards of 18.000 white oak staves for barrels, the value of which will be greatly decreased by the soaking in oil they have received.

There is a chance that the vessel can be hauled off the rocks and towed into the harbor, and an attempt to do this will be made on the first high tide. If she could be brought into smooth water all the oil in barrels now could be saved, and probably nearly all of that broken loose could be pumped out.

The oil was valued at New Orleans at $140,000.00, and insured for $120,000.00 It is of an amber color, in the barrels, and, though so much of it has broken loose, it gives out no odor aboard the ship.

Newport Daily News: April 30, 1891

Yesterday about one hundred and seventy-five barrels of oil were secured from the wreck, but to-day, the lower deck having been opened up, the wreckers are doing better. About one hundred and fifty barrels were brought in this noon and transferred to schooner J. M. Baylies, which sails for Providence this afternoon.

Newport Daily News: May 2, 1891

Yesterday afternoon while engaged in hoisting oil from the stranded ship Lydia Skolfield Mr. Thomas Gaddis, chief diver in the employ of Captain Waters, was struck on the thigh by a swinging cask of oil, and so injured that he was at once brought to this city and taken to the hospital in the ambulance. It was found that his leg was not broken, but was badly bruised, and the knee so injured that he will be unable to work for some time. The accident was one of those unfortunate occurrances liable to happen at any time, the rolling of the ships and the cutting away of the decks making great care necessary in handling the heavy casks.

Today Captain Waters began removing the loose oil floating in the ship Lydia Skolfield, bailing it into the hold of schooner Niantock, which has been fitted to receive it. It was at first intended to pump the floating oil into tanks but it has been decided it could be better removed by bailing and that method is being used. Both steam lighters are busy removing whole barrels.

Newport Daily News: May 4, 1891

Yesterday about two hundred barrels of oil were hoisted from the stranded ship, the heavy sea and strong southerly wind compelling the wreckers to abandon work about 1 o'clock. Today, though it was expected no work could be done on board because of the heavy seas of yesterday, two hundred and two barrels were taken out. Schooner M. A. Piedmore was sent to Providence this morning with a load and schooner J. M. Baylies is loading today. Schooner Menuncatuck succeeded Saturday in hoisting out about fifty barrels of the loose oil from the ship, but owing to the sea yesterday was unable to do anything.

Newport Daily News: May 5, 1891

This morning about two hundred barrels of oil were hoisted out of ship Lydia Skolfield.

Newport Daily News: May 9, 1891

Yesterday tug Aquidneck took schooner Menuncatuck, with about four hundred barrels of loose oil and one hundred whole barrels, to Providence. Tomorrow she will probably take up schooner M. A. Piedmore, loaded with whole barrels. So far about 5,500 whole barrels have been taken from ship Lydia Skolfield, and it is thought there are still about seven hundred on board, the remainder having been broken up. The anchors, chains, and other articles of value on board have been taken off and will be taken to New York by steamer R. J. Merritt, which will probably leave on Tuesday. A considerable portion of the 18,000 white oak staves has also been taken off, and nearly all of this part of the cargo will be saved. The weather has been quite favorable, everything considered, for working at the wreck, though the heavy swell outside has, as it did this morning, often prevented work, when the inner harbor looked like a mill pond.

Newport Daily News: May 12, 1891

Wrecking steamer R. J. Merritt, which has been passing the time at this port since the wreck of ship Lydia Skolfield, has sailed for New York. But little oil in barrels remains on the wreck, only thirty-three barrels having been secured yesterday. The wreckers are busy getting off the white oak staves and the loose oil, a considerable portion of which can be saved.

Newport Daily News: May 18, 1891

The work of saving whole barrels of oil from the wrecked ship, Lydia Skolfield, is practically over, Saturday but four whole barrels being saved. So far 5,957 whole barrels and about 300 loose have been sent to Providence, and Captain Waters now has 107 loose barrels which he will send up at once. This makes a total of 6,364 barrels out of 7,000 on board, secured. Though the amount now daily saved is not large, while the expenses for men, tugs, lighter, etc. remain the same as when large quantities were secured, Captain Waters remains on guard, and will work on the wreck, at the request of the underwriters, as long as any can be saved. Today no work is being done at the wreck because of the heavy sea, and the ship is showing signs of breaking on the port, or shore side, the old break being on the starboard, or offshore side. If this break develops it will not be long before the old ship goes to pieces, and work has to stop, as when once it begins to break, the loose oil will be washed out, and all further attempts at saving it would be useless. Already over nine tenths of the cargo of oil, much more than even the most sanguine had expected, has been saved, and, if the ship remains intact even this excellent record will be surpassed.

Newport Daily News: May 20, 1891

The oil business at Castle Hill had a boom yesterday, when fifty-two whole barrels were secured, and this was continued today, when seventy-five were taken off. These barrels all show signs of the rough time inside the ship, but few have all the hoops on, many have the chimes broken and all are dented and scraped by the floating wreckage. The action of the oil has taken all the paint from the barrels, cleaning the hoops as if they were polished. The oil also has a peculiar action on rubber boots, which are quickly affected and the rubber comes off, as if melted, in a few days. The rubber suits of the divers, made of the best grade of rubber, suffer in the same way, though not to the same extent.

Newport Daily News: May 21, 1891

Tug Aquidneck yesterday brought schooner Menuncatuck from Providence, where she discharged two hundred and forty barrels of loose oil from the Lydia Skolfield. Yesterday one hundred and eight whole barrels in all were taken from the ship.

Newport Daily News: May 23, 1891

Captain Masson of ship Lydia Skolfield, and wife, left for their home, Essex, Connecticut, on the Eolus at 1:30 today. The captain has had the offer of a fine ship in Boston, but has not as yet decided to take command of her. Captain Masson has had command of a ship forty-four years. His attention to the Skolfield and cargo here is praised by all interested.

Newport Daily News: June 4, 1891

The value of the cargo saved from the Brig Lydia Skolfield was $117,486. The value when the vessel struck was $130,000. The persentage saved was the highest ever known in marine insurance circles.

Newport Daily News: July 20, 1891

Ship Lydia Skolfield, which went ashore on the Washbowl, south of Castle Hill, on Sunday, April 19th, went to pieces yesterday afternoon, about 4 o'clock, just as steamer Day Star was turning Beavertail, with an excursion party from Providence. The sides spread, the deck washed ashore and a number of barrels of oil were secured by Mr. Maitland.

Thus ends the saga of the good ship Lydia Skolfield. When we had finished scrutinizing these accounts we did not know whether to rejoice or cry. True, there had been a wreck at Butterball Rock and it was a very large ship but the accounts told us of the large and successful salvage venture. Digging further into the records we surmised that the *Lydia Skolfield* was, indeed, a large ship, almost two hundred feet long, and we

The ill-fated three-masted wooden ship *Lydia Skolfield*, which was wrecked on the rocky shores at the entrance to Narragansett Bay on April 19, 1891. Despite a very successful salvage effort, numerous remains of this vessel can still be found on the sea floor in the vicinity of Castle Hill, Newport, R.I. *Photo courtesy of Peabody Museum, Salem.*

soon came to the conclusion that even if only the hull of a ship of that size remained there must be something to retrieve for an artifact. We immediately began to put together a plan of action and proceeded with our project.

We decided that the best search technique to utilize would be to take the area within which we felt the center of wreckage would lie and grid this area off in fifty foot squares and systematically search out these grids marking them off on a chart which we would draw as the grid progressed. Our search techniques would be somwhat limited as this was the middle of the winter and that would make the use of an underwater sled impossible as we were not equipped with dry suits to withstand the extremely cold water. The circle search technique was proposed but because of the large boulders on the bottom in this area this technique was also discarded as a possibility. We finally had to settle for the free swimming technique using Butterball Rock as the focal point for the grid at least for as long as the water remained frigid. As always, we kept an accurate log of all diving activities at the site and it is through this means that I will illustrate our plan of action, equipment used, and successes.

DIVE #1, Year 1, January 19th—This was the initial dive that we made at the site before we learned the particulars concerning the wreck located here. We chose to dive at night which was a bad choice and we spent our time searching the area immediately around Butterball Rock with very few results. Water temperature was thirty three degrees but at the end of this dive we were even more determined than at the start to get to the bottom of the rumored wreck here.

DIVE #2, January 23rd—Armed now with the name of the vessel and the information gleaned from the newspaper accounts of the disaster we have returned to search out the area between Butterball Rock and the shore. We are now carrying a marker buoy and line each and a hammer for scraping suspicious areas of the bottom. The weather today has been foul but we did manage to locate an anchor chain and some deposits of broken brass spikes. A composite map has been started and we will check our records further to see where the anchor chain we have found comes from.

During the nights between the second dive at the site and the third we spent a great deal of time checking and double checking our records to see where our mistake was in reference to the supposedly salvaged anchor and chain of the *Lydia Skolfield*. We discovered an outstanding fact in this search—the *Lydia Skolfield* was the only one of five different wrecks to have struck the rocks and to have been lost at the southern extremity of Castle Hill. Also to have been totally wrecked here were: schooner *R. B. Glover*—July, 1853; fishing schooner *D. W. Dixon*—April 3, 1856; schooner *Richmond*—February 19, 1859; and schooner *Mattie D.*— January 9, 1886. This put a new light on the search for the remains of the *Lydia Skolfield* and in digging still further through the records we found the one fact that would aid us in our search—of all the vessels wrecked here the *Skolfield* was the only one of which we had knowledge that her bottom was coppered. This was a trick used by early ship builders to foil the attempts of the teredo worm whose main diet was and is a ship's hull timbers. By placing copper sheeting on the bottom of a vessel the worm was stopped from attacking the hull. Now all we had to do was to locate the center of wreckage which had bits of coppering mixed in with the other remains. It sounded very simple but we knew the job would get harder from here on out.

DIVE #3, February 6th—Again we were faced with a foul winter wind and rough sea but we have now determined the best possible point of entry here and we are beginning to become familiar with some of the topographical features of the bottom in this area. Apparently, the buoy that we left to mark the location of the anchor chain previously located has been washed away in the recent winter storms and we could not relocate it on this dive. Water temperature was thirty three degrees.

DIVE #4, February 13th—Our nemesis, foul weather, is still following us whenever we dive here but our composite map is beginning to fill out quite well. We have recovered pieces from at least three different wrecks (one of them a small modern fishing vessel) but as yet nothing we can pinpoint as being from *Skolfield.*

DIVE #5, February 17th—In watching the weather we have concluded that our winter dives on this site will be better done at night as the water and wind conditions seem to be more favorable. Tonight we located a fairly major area of wreckage and recovered several hull spike parts, small nails (maybe the fastenings for the coppering), and some small brass rings (later discovered to be washers for some of the larger spikes). We held a conference right after the dive to work on the composite map and then spent half the night discussing our next dive. We will adapt a small can with a plastic lid for carrying back any small nails that we might find as we have found that they will fall right through the holes in a goody bag.

DIVE #6, February 19th—After only two days, the buoys that we left marking our best spot yet are gone. This was an exasperating dive in search of our previously located site and the combination of foul weather and no luck has brought our morale to an all time low.

DIVE #7, February 20th—We decided that we should search again immediately for the spot we located on DIVE #5 and the weather was slightly more cooperative today. We did not find what we were looking for but we had the opportunity to measure out some distances from one find to another on the bottom to make our composite map more accurate. We are learning to hunt with more success for small artifacts and pieces of artifacts and the limited visibility that we have been dealing with is making our search pattern better as we do not become distracted by trying to look at too large an area of the bottom. We have now superficially covered the area of about two grids.

DIVE #8, February 26th—The weather is turning quite favorable now and we are beginning to find many areas in which there are a considerable number of fused iron objects. Many small nails and partial spikes are beginning to show themselves more and it seems likely that since we are diving in relatively shallow water (twenty feet or less) the changes in wind direction have some effect on the appearance of artifacts on the bottom apparently from shifting sand pockets in this area.

DIVE #9, February 27th—We have decided to try to physically grid the bottom in the area previously searched and I ran a line of approximately one hundred foot length from a buoy we dropped just southeast of Ragged Point to a new find made today. This was a day of many finds and we made three important notes of interest: 1) Two I-beams of iron or steel were located and buoyed near the rock (one runs northeast to southwest and the other runs southeast to northwest); 2) There are a large number of crevices running southwest to northeast with many small items in them; and 3) Various sand pockets were found with many partial spikes and nails. We think we are very close to the center of wreckage now but there is still no conclusive evidence that this wreckage belongs to the *Lydia Skolfield.*

DIVE #10, March 2nd—Finally a break in the search for the *Skolfield* remains—today we both located and recovered pieces of coppering from what has to be the remains of our wreck. We have culminated our search and have become successful wreck hunters and our finds of spikes, nails and washers from the wreckage has made the hunt well worth it. I have developed a theory which should have occurred to me several dives ago—the sand pockets which have been yielding little bits and pieces of the wreck all along are the key to the entire wealth of artifacts. The "Crevice Theory" is that the heaviest objects to land in a rock crevice will work their way to the bottom of these sand filled pockets while the lighter objects will lie on top or be buried just under the sand in the crevice. Checking this out with some crevice searches proved this theory to be a sound one.

DIVE #11, March 6th—Our base line set on the bottom on DIVE #9 is completely gone but our buoys for the major area of wreckage are intact and we anxiously returned to search the outlying areas around what we feel is definitely the center of wreckage of the *Lydia Skolfield* with some interesting results. I located an iron object just east southeast of the rock itself which is semicircular or crescent shaped with an arm like a piston rod and spokes attached. I don't think this is wreckage from the *Skolfield* but I intend to look into my references on marine engine construction to see if the piece can be identified. We are trying a new method of fanning the sand pockets by the use of ping pong paddles and if you should choose to try it—good luck—weighted or unweighted paddles make little difference. A significant artifact that was retrieved today appears to be a door latch and is a fine artifact indeed.

After this dive we held another conference and decided that although we were becoming considerably successful of late we would suspend diving operations at this site for awhile as the interest among other local divers was becoming ever more evident and we did not wish the area ravaged by a mass of brass hungry divers. We would definitely return to the site when the outside interests dwindled somewhat but for now we were satisfied with our success.

DIVE #12, June 17th—Sometimes I think the weather is out to protect this wreck from the eyes of serious wreck hunters. Our first trip back in three months and although we got right back into the area of wreckage the unfavorable weather and sea conditions made the dive only a fair one with few spikes and some nails recovered.

DIVE #13, June 19th—Visibility improving; working slightly to the east and south of the rock in the vicinity of the center of wreckage. An amazing find has been made here which almost positively identifies this area as the wreckage of the *Lydia Skolfield*—a nickel whose date is 188?. This is probably the most conclusive evidence yet found that would belong to a wreck of 1891 vintage. Also, I recovered a fourteen inch long intact brass spike in the wreckage here which makes us laugh at all the partial spikes we have picked up heretofore thinking that there would be no intact spikes left. We have noted that the percentage of wood that remains in the wreck is probably less than three per cent and that is buried beneath the sandy areas here.

DIVE #14, June 22nd—Today was the day to test out another theory which now appears so logical that I don't know how we could have missed it before. The prevailing wind and sea here is southwest and in its ever present push to the northeast (or shoreward) the only place that an object would stop would have to be where it was sheltered from the surge, i.e., in a crevice or on the northeast or lee side of any large rock in the area. Checking this out proved this to be the case, indeed, and today's finds included several intact spikes, hoards of coppering nails, and a brass key. This is perhaps the nicest artifact that I have personally recovered during all our diving here.

DIVE #15, September 11th—Another fine dive in the area northeast of Butterball Rock brought to light several more intact spikes varying from eight to fourteen inches in length. We are completely satisfied now with the wreck and the area in general. We still leave the wreck alone again for awhile as interest is again being picked up in the area and any further finds of importance must wait.

DIVE #16, Year 2, April 30th—Again we visit one of our favorite and easily accessible wreck sites and once again it has proven to be a good dive. Working to the north of the center of wreckage I picked up a strangely shaped piece of brass which we cannot as yet identify. Several more spikes came to light and so many nails that we have stopped retrieving all but the intact ones.

DIVE #17, May 31st—At last we have decided to use the underwater sled in this area and see what else will turn up but the large amount of bottom growth made this an impossible task. The center of wreckage of the as yet unidentified modern vessel lost here has been located by two of our divers south of the rock and deserves some further investigation at a later date.

After several more average dives on the wrecksite one more theory had come to mind and was tested very successfully on DIVE #20 at the site.

DIVE #20, August 2nd—I have decided that even on an apparently rocky bottom there can be dense objects to be found even below the level of the bottom. On this assumption I decided to take a section of the bottom where there were only iron objects found and dig until I reached the real bottom and either found artifacts or grew tired of digging. It took quite a while but when about eighteen inches below the bottom I hit the jackpot. In one hole alone I recovered thirteen intact spikes ranging from three inches in length to eight inches in length. There may be more important artifacts to be turned up in this manner but that will be a long project which would be best aided by an air lift.

Since DIVE #20 we have returned to the wreck of the *Lydia Skolfield* for approximately a dozen more dives with each new dive revealing more historical evidence of an era that is gone but not forgotten. Although no more spectacular finds have been made than have already been mentioned we return to this wreck often (particularly during the winter months when the boats are out of the water) and look forward to each dive as a new adventure which may sometime yield more coins or even a super surprise artifact not now imagined. We have amassed since this project began dozens of intact spikes, hundreds of partial spikes, thousands of coppering nails, several brass washers, one coin, a brass key, a brass door hinge, a brass door handle, and several other interesting brass objects which are as yet unidentified.

As almost all of the artifacts recovered from the wreck have been of non-ferrous metal the problem of preservation has been minimal. One iron piece recovered here was of several links of chain from another wreck in the vicinity and by coating it thoroughly with varnish it has retained its fine condition for nearly five years. Wooden sections have been spotted but as yet none have been retrieved to my knowledge as they would be quite fragile after a period of almost eighty years underwater.

Wrecks of this type literally dot the coastal areas of the continental United States (particularly on the northeastern coastline) and it is very evident that they have much to offer the ambitious wreck searcher who can seek out and discover a wreck of this caliber and vintage on an extremely slim budget. Of a more difficult nature are wrecks of a much earlier vintage such as the Spanish brig *Minerva* lost just after the turn of the 18th century and to be discussed next.

6 Minerva

WE discussed in Chapter 1 the procedure to use when researching a marine disaster in a logical order. However, from time to time wrecks are discovered in an inverse manner—working from the actual location of the wrecksite backwards to identify the particular wreck that you have located. Such was the case with the Spanish brig *Minerva* which was located shortly after diving operations began on the *Lydia Skolfield*. This type of wreck searching is very difficult as you will see and putting the pieces of the puzzle together to identify your wrecksite although highly challenging is not recommended.

It all began with a dive we made in search of a 20th century fishing vessel lost near one of the local spearfishing spots in our area. Actually it began with the recovery of a brass gate valve found while snorkeling in this area. My spearfishing partner and I immediately had our interest aroused at this find and a check through the growing wreck file that we were compiling showed that this artifact could be from one of several ships lost in this area. This was to begin a bizarre search for one of these wrecks which culminated in the accidental location of the *Minerva* and, with a lot of luck and hard work, the identification of this wrecksite to be that of this vessel.

DIVE #1, Year 1, July 23rd—We came in search of a modern fishing vessel from which I have retrieved a brass gate valve while snorkeling and to our utter amazement we have discovered at least two very old iron cannon. We cannot believe that we have been so lucky as to stumble on the remains of a really old vessel and we will immediately begin to formulate a plan of action to retrieve at least one cannon and to identify the wreck.

As soon as our feet touched the shore after this dive we made immediate plans for a conference to discuss the possible methods of retrieving our find. Although both of us have had some experience in lifting small artifacts, neither of us had ever attempted to retrieve anything of this size and magnitude. We soon made arrangements to use (on a testing basis for a friend) a commercially designed five hundred pound lift bag and a heavy duty flexible rubber container to raise our first cannon.

DIVE #2, July 24th—We have decided to take a good close look at this wrecksite to see what other artifacts may lie in the area but due to a severe current and a large amount of bottom growth searching here will be an extremely difficult task. After using a set of doubles we have found no more artifacts than we knew were here before.

We decided to proceed with our cannon retrieval as soon as possible in the hopes that it would provide a clue as to the nature of the wreck, i.e., its nationality, age, size, etc. The problems, we were to learn, were about to begin but we proceeded ahead at full steam with nothing but visions of immense success. A search through the local records brought absolutely nothing to light. All that we had to work with was the fact that the use of cannon aboard sailing ships was phased out during the period around the 1840s. Early records of the Newport area were somewhat hard to come by and would take time to be searched and an unfortunate gap in the records was found covering the period of the Revolutionary War when Newport was occupied by the British forces. We were quite sure that our wreck was of Revolutionary War vintage based on intuition and the fact that the cannon looked that old. Actually we had no idea of the exact age of the wreck but we hoped that it would prove to be of significant historical value.

At about 3:00 a.m. on the morning of the 25th I awoke to a phone call from my teammate who said conditions were ideal with a dense fog bank over the entire Newport area. We agreed to meet at the site at 6 o'clock each of us using his own boat and bringing plenty of extra tools. It was no easy task navigating through the fog to the site but by 6:10 A.M. we were both anchored over the wreck checking all of our tools and preparing for our water entry. Our tools for the job consisted of two brick hammers, a chisel, a large crowbar, fifty feet of parachute cord, a length of quarter-inch polypropelene line, and a five hundred pound lift bag. As we entered the water to begin our most ambitious project yet we could not help but think of the contribution that we were about to make to marine history. We attacked the uppermost cannon with an enthusiasm known only to a wreck diver. The cannon we chose was fused to the bottom with such a grip as to make us feel that King Neptune himself refused to give up this prize to men of the surface world. We tunneled under the barrel and quickly attached the parachute cord at what we hoped would be the balancing point and fastened the lift bag to this mass of lines. Filling the lift bag slowly we watched as it balooned out and began to rise putting a strain on our prize. We worked with the hammers and crowbar to free the barrel from the rocks to which it was fused but it seemed a hopeless task. We filled the lift bag to capacity but it didn't budge our prize. There seemed to be only one final point to which the cannon grasped the bottom but a check with out submersible guages showed that we were both running out of air and must return to the boats for more tanks. We had already spent more than two hours of bottom time on this project but we knew that it would only be a short time before we would see our lift bag floating on the surface with the cannon barrel suspended beneath it. After chipping away at the rocky bottom for about twenty minutes more the cannon suddenly leapt for the surface. It was freed of Neptune's grasp once and for all. Unfortunately, if flew upward with such a momentum that it caused the lift bag to broach, dumping its air, and as quickly as it had flown to the surface the cannon fell again to the ocean floor. Undaunted, we checked our lines and reinflated the lift bag which again brought the cannon barrel to the surface although this time it hung in a vertical position. We returned all of the tools to the boats and I took the rubber float to attach it to the lowest end of the barrel to lift the cannon back into a horizontal position. It was in inflating this float that we discovered that it was not a circular float as we had thought but a flat "pancake" seat for a rubber raft. It did not provide much lift but every little bit would help and we decided to use it anyway. Returning to the boats we were elated at our success so far. Our job now was to tow this prize about three miles to the nearest davit which was at the local Coast Guard station and whose use had been arranged for by the simple barter system. We agreed to catch a bag full of lobsters for the men at the station in return for the use of the davit to haul our artifact out of the water. Towing the four hundred and fifty pound cannon with a fourteen foot skiff powered by a ten horse outboard was quite a job and four hours later we had still not arrived at the Coast Guard station. At about 5:00 p.m. we arrived and after dropping the barrel to the bottom and resetting the hauling lines we brought to light our most historical artifact yet. It was not yet time to celebrate, however, as we had to transport our prize to its new home to be preserved for future visitors to admire. The exact process for preserving this find had not yet been determined but we knew that the oxidation process would begin as soon as we took it out of the salt water so our first move would be to reimmerse it into water until the correct chemical process could be determined. I immediately began construction of a plywood box over six feet long and about eighteen inches wide and deep to store our find in and although I sealed this box to prevent leakage it quickly leaked anyway. We decided that it would be best to bury the cannon to at least slow the oxidation process until we could find a proper vat or make one. Our find was indeed a good one. Almost completely intact except for a section of the iron at the muzzle of the barrel, it had two excellent trunnions and a decently preserved breech and button. The trunnions when cleaned of the three eights of an inch thick layer of calcareous growth showed two fine trunnion markings which would aid us greatly later in identifying the origin and age of the barrel.

We had decided previously that since there were two of us involved in this particular project we would raise two cannon and now our task was to formulate a better plan of action for raising and transporting the second cannon. We had learned much from our first endeavor of cannon raising: 1) that the object being raised must be free of the bottom before it is to be lifted to the surface; 2) that the commercially developed lift bag is convenient but it is not the best means for raising large and bulky objects as there is no way to seal the air inside the bag to prevent the possibility of its broaching; and 3) that to tow the object behind a boat is not the most efficient means to transport it from the wrecksite to the shore. We decided that for the second cannon raising we would take a large pry bar to insure that the cannon, if fused to the bottom, would be free of the bottom before any lifting was done. For a lifting device we chose a fifty five gallon oil drum which could lift approximately four hundred and fifty pounds and instead of towing the cannon back to shore we decided to try and sling it underneath the boat to cut down the amount of surface area being dragged through the water.

Our first opportunity to raise the second cannon came only one short week later when conditions were almost identical to those of the first trip out. On this attempt we took a photographer to record the event as we were confident that this time we had the system down pat. Our water entry was about 8:00 A.M. on this day and as we cruised over the wrecksite we were surprised but pleased to find that directly beneath the first cannon that we had removed lay another slightly smaller one. This cannon appeared to be in better condition than the one which we had chosen to remove so we made an on-the-site decision to remove this one instead. The work on this cannon proceeded much more swiftly and smoothly than in our previous operation as we were now experienced cannon retrievers and in a very short time we had the cannon ready for lifting. The procedure which we had devised for moving the oil drum to the site was extremely simple even though the barrel is a large and bulky object. The two holes in the drum were sealed and a rope attached to it to be taken to the object to be raised. By pulling the rope around the cannon barrel the empty drum was floated to a spot directly over the artifact and by unscrewing the caps and flooding the barrel it sank right next to the cannon. We had rigged a harness to the barrel and attached a large shackle below it. After tethering the cannon and attaching it to the drum we simply filled the drum through the smaller hole (allowing the water to escape through the larger hole) and watched it gently rise to the surface. We were amazed at how much simpler this job was with an oil drum instead of a tipsy lift bag. On the surface we added more air to the drum until all the water was removed and replaced the caps to prevent any leakage of air and then towed it over to the boat. We had purposely suspended the barrel vertically this time and before entering the boat fastened a line to the lower end of the tube and passed it underneath the boat and over the opposite rail. Entering the boat and doffing our gear took only minutes and then the hard work began. We fastened a line to the parachute cord where the shackle was attached and by putting a strain on this line we were able to unfasten the shackle and remove the drum from the cannon. After fastening that line to a cleat within the boat we began to take a strain on the line to the other end of the barrel. After tugging for about ten minutes we felt that we could pull the cannon no higher and we fastened this line to another cleat in the boat. I put on my mask and jumped over the side to check the status of the cannon and it seemed perfectly fine but a little lower than we had anticipated. We decided that if we were to do this again we could use a come-along to bring the object up even higher. Pleased with ourselves, we set off on the journey to shore again and amazingly this time the entire trip took us only about one hour instead of five! We repeated the process with the davit as this part of the operation had worked well the first time. After transporting this cannon to its new resting place I noticed that the yard was beginning to look like our own Boot Hill with piles of dirt, like graves, sitting ominously as the sun set on another fine day of wreck diving.

By now our project had attracted some local attention and we were becoming quite leery of returning to this site in the near future. We decided to let things quiet down a bit before resuming our search for even greater artifacts from this historical wrecksite. In the meantime, we had a lot of work to do. There were two major projects still ahead of us: 1) the preservation of the two cannon barrels and their final display; and 2) the identification of the wreck that we had found to complete the record of this fascinating experience. Since the preservation of the cannon was the most critical project at hand I quickly began searching far and wide for all the available information relative to preservation of artifacts. While doing this I was puzzled as to the best possible type of vat to use in setting up a chemical bath and I finally decided that a metal vat would be best. Through the assistance of several friends I finally procured a two hundred and seventy five gallon oil drum which, when cut in half lengthwise, served amply as a fine container in which to set up the chemical solution. As I continued to hunt for the ideal preservative solution I also worked on the positive identification of the cannon. The cannon with the growth removed both measured fifty four inches in length, the outside muzzle diameter of cannon #1 was approximately seven inches, the bore of that cannon was two and one half inches, the trunnion shoulders measured approximately four inches square and the trunnion diameters were each two and one half inches. Cannon #1 weighed approximately four hundred to four hundred and fifty pounds. Both weapons had four reinforcing rings and were constructed of black iron. Apparently, neither is definitely British as they do not have the common broad arrow or GR marking on the upper portion of the breech. That much I knew about cannon but I was about to learn much more.

I quickly learned that the discovery of a cannon is not such an unusual occurrence as we had thought. There is even a Cannon Hunters Association of Seattle (better known as CHAOS) whose membership is made up of people interested in finding and preserving old cannon. This put a slight damper on our discovery but we still felt that our accomplishment was great as these cannon must be very old and they were, after all, recovered from a wrecksite.

Finally, the preservative process I had been waiting for came to light and step two of this project was about to begin. The process was described in Chapter 4 in some detail and the task now was to acquire almost two hundred pounds of sodium hydroxide and zinc chips and to set up the bath. As more time went by and we awaited the delivery of the chemicals I became quite a bit more familiar with the identification of cannon and my library expanded slightly with several good books concerning these smooth bore artillery pieces. Several knowledgeable persons tentatively identified the cannon as of British origin despite the lack of a broad arrow. We suddenly had a breakthrough, or so we thought, when other members of our diving team recovered some smaller cannon from the site one of which was distinctly marked with a *fleur de lis* on the barrel which definitely is not of British origin. Soon the chemicals arrived and the chemical bath was ready to go. We encountered an extremely large problem in moving the cannon from their temporary home to the vat but finally through the use of a portable A-frame and a come-along we were able to get the cannon into the vat and place it in an out of the way place for the preservation process to work. There they sat in solution number one while I have endeavored to find an inexpensive means to acquire mossy zinc and a large quantity of distilled water for the baths to say nothing of an oven large enough to bake them in. To anyone who is interested in such a project I can only advise you that it is very expensive and an arduous task to undertake.

After several months and hundreds of inquiries I began to get on the right track as far as the identification of cannon #1 through the trunnion markings. With the aid of the staff of the Smithsonian Institution in Washington, D.C. I procured a series of illustrations of trunnion markings which showed the exact markings on one of the trunnions of cannon #1. According to that information there was a very good chance that the gun had been cast in Sweden! I quickly contacted the company in Sweden (still in existence!) which supposedly had cast the cannon and after several months received a fine letter concerning them and confirming the fact that at least one of the cannon had been cast there between the years 1772 and 1831. This news was excellent as it placed the date of the wreck as sometime after 1772 which could indeed make this a wreck of Revolutionary War vintage. The company also sent a detailed brochure of the history of the company with much information concerning the manufacture of early cannon and the processes involved. If only I could read Swedish I'm sure it would make great reading but then you can't win them all and the people had been very friendly and cooperative.

Another important item of interest had come to light about this time which made our researching very much easier. We had been preceeding under the assumption that the vessel was Swedish and of early 19th century vintage when we learned that it was not only not uncommon but it was, in fact, quite common for ships of different nations to be carrying guns from different countries on board at all times. This was because of the value of a cannon in early times. Many countries bought or captured guns from other countries and rather than throw them overboard they would keep them as their own if they were needed. This fact left us now with an imprecise date and totally unknown nationality for our wreck and piqued our interest to an even greater extent.

We had been pondering the question for almost a year when in one dive the mystery was almost totally cleared up with the recovery of a really super artifact—a piece of eight! A Spanish *reale* cast in Santiago, Chile in 1811 in almost mint condition was recovered by one of our divers cemented to a cluster of several cannon balls and musket balls. This was indeed a super find because it gave us a much smaller span of time in which the wreck probably occurred. With a renewed vigor the search through the local records was begun again and in short order we had found a new lead to the identity of this remarkable wreck. While working on this new lead on the research end of the project we started to dive in the area of the wrecksite again. Although we had some visions of finding more coins we did not look at this wreck as a treasure wreck from that standpoint. We have all had our share of get rich quick dreams and our divers understand that the real value of an early shipwreck is the historical knowledge we can bring back for future historians to study and learn from. In fact, we did not recovery any more coins from the wreck at that time and perhaps never will but the spikes, cannon balls, and other small artifacts have continued to keep our interest in this fine wreck at a high level. We made the decision at this point to continue our silence concerning the exact location of this wreck so that treasure hunting divers would not scour the area destroying the flora and fauna here and destroy any further historical remains in search of large quantities of gold or silver which probably don't exist on this wreck anyway. We have refrained

Pictured here is the Brig *Caravan*, of Salem, which closely resembles the Brig *Minerva*, which was lost off the shores of Rhode Island in 1812. *Photo courtesy of Peabody Museum, Salem.*

from diving in this area for several years now and only when we feel the area is safe from scavengers will we return to do an extensive survey of this historical site.

The story of the shipwreck itself now came completely to light through the early records of our ancestors and, as is the case with many a fine wreck, the story behind the disaster makes fascinating reading.

It was in the month of December in the year 1812 that the little brig *Minerva* found herself plying the coastal waters of New England on her latest voyage from Havana bound to Bristol, R.I. with an assorted cargo of general merchandise including rum, Catalonian wine, and iron. It had been a rough voyage for all and the crew were anxiously awaiting the chance to go ashore and rest (particularly with the advent of the Christmas holidays close at hand). The Master, Angel Cifuenter, was aware of the low level of morale in his crew but continued to command the vessel in his usual businesslike manner. Secretly he felt as the men did that the holiday season was no time to work but he was being well paid to carry cargo between these two ports and carry it he would.

By the 20th of December, somewhere off the Virginia capes, a very violent storm had caught his ship and followed it right through the last hours of the vessel's existence. It was Monday, December 24th, Christmas Eve, and throughout Newport the townspeople were cheerful and gay at this happy time of the year though the storm that had followed Captain Cifuenter raged all about them. When within sight of land and a chance of shore leave the crew of the Minerva became much relieved that the ten day voyage from Havana was almost over but before they could travel as little as one mile further their vessel, heavily laden, struck bottom on an outcropping of rocks and held fast, the sea making a complete breach over her. The heavy winds and blinding snow made the vessel almost invisible from shore even if anyone had known just where to look for it. The crewmen quickly scrambled into the rigging, sure that this voyage was having a tragic end; and they were right, for although the captain fired one of the eight cannon aboard as a signal of distress to attract attention to his ship's perilous position, the townspeople ignored it as being the signalling fire from one of the New York packet ships on this festive occasion. Who knows how many hours the men spent in the rigging in the frigid winter storm that could only be termed a Northeaster before they fell, one by one, to the icy waters below them? On a section of the ship torn loose in the fury of the storm the boatswain and nine members of the crew managed to get to shore and safety while leaving the captain, mate, and seven others of the crew behind. The devastating effect of the storm was as effective as ever in reducing the ship to a pile of tinder and splinters in a matter of hours.

The bodies of the lost crewmen were washed ashore during the next week along with three pipes of rum and eight casks of Catalonian wine—all else was given up to the sea. The bodies recovered were decently interred in the Old Collin's Burial Grounds close by. From that day forward the use of cannon as a signal of anything but distress was suspended by all sea captains in the immediate vicinity.

7 *Llewellyn Howland*

U P till now we had spent most of our time and effort in searching for
wrecks of sailing vessels which lay in quite shallow water and we
had decided that our next search would be for a more modern vessel of
steel construction and in somewhat deeper water. Delving into our mass
of research material we came up with what seemed like a fine possibility in
the vicinity—the two hundred and eighty three foot long steel tanker
Llewellyn Howland lost in the area of Seal Ledge, off Newport, on April
21, 1924. As we proceeded to read the accounts of this disaster a fantastic
story unfolded which was to lead us to this fine representative of a
modern shipwreck.

Newport Daily News: April 21, 1924

TANKER STRIKES ROCKS
Crew and Luggage Landed By Coast Guard Power Boat
Quantities of Oil Coming From Vessel,
Which Thought She was Sailing in Deep Water.

In the bright sunshine this morning, with air so rarified that vision
was unusually good, tanker Llewellyn Howland of the Bayland Line
struck hard and fast on submerged rocks about a mile off the Brenton
Reef Coast Guard Station. This noon the crew and their luggage were
landed by the Coast Guard in their power boat. The bottom of the
tanker must be badly torn as all her fires soon died and oil in quantities
is coming from the vessel's tanks.

The ship is under charter to the New England Oil Company, and
sailed from the refining works at Fall River this morning, with 26,000
barrels of oil for the International Paper Company, to be discharged at
Portland, Maine. After clearing the lightship she headed eastward, and
it appears crowded the coastline too hard. According to one of the crew
who was brought ashore, Captain Larson of the ship said his chart
showed a great deal more water at the point than there is, and it would
seem from remarks of the crew that it was supposed that the ship was

Except for the name (the *San Eduardo*, of Newcastle, England), this steamer could be the tanker *Llewellyn Howland*. Although a far cry from the supertanker of today, tankers of this size carried a significant quantity of oil that could easily cause extensive damage in the days when control of the released oil was nearly impossible. *Photo courtesy of Peabody Museum, Salem.*

sailed where there were fathoms of water, rather than only a similar number of feet.

The ship went on at 10:43, with such a bump that it toppled the crew off their feet, and then plowed ahead on the ledge, becoming hard fixed. Engines were reversed and a strenuous effort was made to back off, but she would not budge, while the water poured into the ship, drowning the fires and stalling any further attempt to work off. The oil tanks were also punctured, and the black mass soon covered the water all around. Under the southwest wind the rocks along shore will soon be stained up as was the freshly painted life boat and the crew who went out on her. Under the light sea running, the ship is rolling some in the cradle of rocks on which she rests, and this will do her no good.

Captain Larson and his two mates remained on board after the crew's dunnage had been placed in one of the ship's boats, and the other members of the ship's company had boarded the power life boat. They are in no immediate danger, but the ship is in a bad place in case of an offshore storm. Under the conditions of the forenoon, it was a rather tame rescue, with none of the exciting experiences or sufferings from the weather which frequently mark rescues from wrecks.

• • •

The ship has gone on the head of the reef near No. 2 buoy, and one of the men upon coming ashore telephoned the refinery in Fall River, where he was informed that it would send down relief, including a barge to salvage what of the oil can be pumped out. This will greatly lighten the ship, but thus far there has been no opportunity to carry on an examination to determine the extent of her injuries, and what will have to be done to pull her off.

Newport Daily News: April 22, 1924

TANKER MAY BREAK UP
Heavy Seas Causing Her To Suffer Sorely On Rocks
Appears To Have Taken A List To Starboard
And To Be Settling By The Stern

Heavy seas, rising since she went on the rocks, are causing oil tanker Llewellyn Howland to suffer sorely as she lies on Seal Ledge, off the south shore. No one was left on the ship last night and this morning no attempt was made to board her, as there was nothing that could be done.

• • •

This noon observations indicated that the ship might not live until the present seas abate. The view of the vessel is not of the best at any time, but as there are rifts in the dense atmosphere the watchers in the tower catch a glimpse of her. She appears to be settling by the stern, and oil seems to be coming out from aft. She appeared to the crew yesterday as having run up on the ledge until she was supported amidships, and when her position appeared to have been changed this morning they thought she might be swinging on a pivot, as it were. The seas have increased since daylight and this noon it was stated that she was receiving a terrible pounding. Boatswain's Mate Fitzsimmons said he was glad all hands were off her. She is a ship that will stand a terrible amount of pounding, as she was built in the days when they really built. A plate in her engine room states that she was built by the Morgan Iron Works in 1888. She is of iron, not steel, and her ribs are particularly close together.

Yesterday afternoon officials came from the company's plant at Fall River. The fireroom force was orcered back on board to try to start up fires to operate the oil pumps, that the oil might be pumped into the tank barge being sent down from Fall River. This barge is now anchored in the harbor here. The Coast Guard took the officials and the firemen on board, and after making a survey of the craft it was determined that nothing could be done and all hands left the ship. The survey resulted in the determination that the pumps could not be used, because the suction pumps were ruptured.

• • •

Captain Larson maintains that he laid a course which should have given his ship plenty of water, had Buoy No. 2 been in proper position. The government will now determine whether the buoy has drifted from its proper location.

The ship was built years ago for the German Standard Oil Company and this was her first trip with cargo since an extensive overhauling in New York.

• • •

A representative of the Boyland Line and an underwriter arrived here today and preparations were at once made to pay off the crew, to make a wreck report and a marine protest, formalities which follow regularly such an accident. Some of the men left for Boston and some for Portland, Maine this afternoon.

Newport Daily News: April 23, 1924

TANKER APPEARS FATED
Stern Seems To Have Settled And Possibly The Bow
Observations Indicate That
Wreckers Will Not Be Able To Save The Craft

Tanker Llewellyn Howland appears to be fated to rest in a grave on Seal Ledge. This morning, when the Coast Guard began to make observations through the glasses, they found the stern to have settled below the surface. The bow appeared also to have settled though they were unable to tell if there had been any lift of the bow along with the settling of the stern. The settling of the stern may mean that her back is broken and that the steamer is breaking in two. The settling of the bow may mean that the heavy pounding may be breaking up the hull where it rests on the ledge and that the upper works are settling down as the underbody crumples under the disintegrating apparently taking place.

• • •

The Coast Guard cutter which was here yesterday has sailed again, as her captain concluded that his ship could do nothing for the stranded vessel and the tank barge which was brought here to take the oil has also gone along. Not even the Coast Guard lifeboat has been out to the craft since Monday afternoon, when it took the captain off, as when daylight came yesterday morning the seas were rolling so high that nothing could be done, and since then they have been increasing instead of diminishing.

The oil is without doubt defiling the rocks and beaches along shore to such an extent that it will be a long while before it wears off, but the heavy surf is throwing the oil up on the rocks in some places where there are depressions which for the past two years have been oiled by hand, in the mosquito elimination fight.

There seems to be some agitation in town, on theory that Newport should rise in force against the defiling of its shores and that the company should be made to go out and pump into tanks what oil is left in the ship. On the other hand, it appears to be an "Act of God" that is spreading the oil along shore and maritime men cannot see that it is within the power of any human agency to go out and prevent the oil going to waste. From present indications, the entire cargo of oil will leak out of the tanks before wreckers are able to go alongside to do anything.

This morning Mayor Sullivan went around the Ocean Drive to see the wreck, and more particularly to see the damage to the shores by the cargo of oil which is spreading in all directions, from Beavertail Light eastward to Buzzard's Bay. Upon his return to his office he telegraphed to the New England Oil Company in Fall River, and while regretting the loss desired immediate assurance that the remaining cargo would be pumped from the wreck.

• • •

Newport Daily News: April 24, 1924

SHORES TO BE PROTECTED
Engineer Corps Will Blow Up Wreck, Lacking Action
Management Of Company Directed To Proceed—
Not Much Chance For Salvage

Assurances were given today that every effort will be made to stay as much as possible further damage to the shores from the presence of the stranded oil tanker. Mayor Sullivan was informed by Major Peterson of the U.S. Engineer Corps of this district that he had conferred with the company officials relative to salvaging the oil, and informed them that if they do not act promptly the wreck will be blown up by the government, thus having the trouble over as soon as possible. He has also been informed that the Board of Purification of State Waters and the State Harbor Commission will do what they can.

Before noon today the Chamber of Commerce officials were convinced that their gun fire had hit bull's eyes. They had aimed at the directors of the oil company, to save Newport's shores, and reached them. Mr. Max Agassiz and the president of the First National Bank of Boston sent word that they had reached directors, who had informed them that the management of the company would be directed to proceed expeditiously to prevent whatever further damage to the shores may be possible.

Mr. Gurney of Providence representing the insurance underwriters, visited stranded tanker Llewellyn Howland this morning, and before leaving for home stated that he did not see much for salvage. The ship has been swung on the rocks and this morning does not appear to be more than fifty feet outside buoy No. 2. Her stern is well under water and her bow is raised.

The sea was fairly smooth this morning, but by noon it had ruffled up so that the wreckers would be unable to work about her, were they here with their plant. The wrecking representative who dropped around to look over the situation, and all others connected with the ship, have departed and apparently the company has consigned the whole matter to the insurance companies, to do as they like.

• • •

Appeals for relief have been sent out in every direction but all they bring back is promises to do what they can, and this is not very assuring. At present the Chamber of Commerce is making a drive on the directors of the New England Oil Company, through intimate acquaintances who have estates here, which will suffer from further distribution of oil in these waters.

• • •

With oil cheap, and ships today a drug on the market, it is easily seen that there is not likely to be much incentive to engage in wrecking operations, especially difficult ones. In anything like calm weather it would be comparatively easy to empty the tanks in eight or ten hours, could the ship's pumps be used, but with the suction lines shattered and most of the tanks underwater, the proposition is entirely different. At present there are so many unknown qualities in the problem that men acquainted with such matters are unwilling to offer a suggestion as to what can be done.

Pressed for an opinion as to how much oil remained in the ship, a wrecker yesterday ventured a guess that perhaps two of the eight tanks were ruptured. Should this be the true state of affairs, the shores of the Rhode Island coast and Narragansett Bay have received but little of the black grease at present.

Boatswain's Mate Fitzsimmons stated that this morning after visiting the ship it was impossible to say what tanks were intact, but that little oil appears to be leaking away at present. He went out with Mr. Gurney, and it was the first visit made to the scene since last Monday afternoon, and the first chance to make even a casual survey of the craft since she was pounded by the heavy seas. He says that, from such view as could be taken this morning, it was impossible to tell what, if any, tanks are still intact, and ventured the thought that if the forward tank is intact it is the only one that can be emptied at present, with any like reasonable effort.

Newport Daily News: April 25, 1924

SUMMER PEOPLE ACTIVE
Endeavoring To Save Further Damage From Oil Tanker—
Sea Quiet And Ship Has Drifted Close To Buoy
With Deep Water Alongside

Telegrams are being received in number by the Chamber of Commerce from owners of summer estates, which indicate that they are active in an endeavor to have something done to save further damage by oil from stranded tanker Llewellyn Howland.

All appears to be in the air as to who is to proceed and how to proceed. The matter is being discussed in Washington, at the state capitol and in financial circles. No one knows how much oil there is still in the vessel to ooze out, and no one desires the oil now, except to have it kept off the Rhode Island shores. A wrecker reports that there is no equity in either ship or cargo, and suggests that the easiest way to remove the wreck is to set fire to it, but it is admitted that this may be a serious undertaking. In the deliberations of various state offices, Governor Flynn has injected the statement that the situation requires prompt and drastic action and that action should be taken to wipe out the menace, as a fire department would a conflagration. The governor has taken the position that this is no time to discuss who or what is what, but there should be action. On the other hand, about every agency—government, state and financial—has been pleading lack of jurisdiction.

This morning two representatives came from the New England Oil Works in Fall River and made a general survey of the wreck, but left no information as to what was to be done.

Boatswain's Mate Fitzsimmons reports this morning that the sea is fairly quiet and that he has been out to the ship, which has drifted even closer to the buoy. By soundings he has established the fact that there is sixteen to eighteen feet of water on the lee side of the tanker, which suggests that light-drafted craft can approach near-by, to work. In a quiet sea her stern is exposed at low water.

Newport Daily News: April 28, 1924

TO CONFER AS TO TANKER
Major Peterson, Of Engineers, Ordered To Washington
State Board Requests Government
To Assume Work Of Removing Menace

The vessel and cargo of stranded tanker Llewellyn Howland, having been abandoned as announced in Saturday's Daily News through the activities of the Board of Purification of State Waters, Major Peterson of the U.S. Enginner Office in Providence has been ordered to Washington to confer with the officers there. The securement of the formal abandonment of a ship and cargo in less than a week is something of a record in itself, and came about through extraordinary pressure and activities of almost everyone who could lend a hand.

• • •

The problem of how to dispose of the oil without further defacing the shores is a difficult one. In the minds of experts who have already studied the problem and on the file of Congress there is said to be a bill which anticipated a nuisance of this kind and which will force companies who are shipping oil by water to be responsible for damage caused by its escape removing the possibility of quitting when they find that the salvage would be more expensive than to stand the loss by deserting their property.

• • •

According to report from Washington, Congressman Burdick has already conferred with General Harry Taylor, Assistant Chief of Engineers, with the result that Major Peterson would report in Washington for a conference today with representatives of several departments to do with maritime affairs with a view to finding a solution of the problem.

Newport Daily News: April 29, 1924

ENGINEER OFFICE IS GIVEN POWER TO ACT
Awaits British Underwriters To Remove Oil Menace
—SPECIAL TO THE NEWS—

Washington, April 29th: Officials of the War Department, including Secretary Weeks and General Harry Taylor, Assistant Chief of Engineers, today conferred with Major V. L. Peterson of the U.S. Engineer Office in Providence regarding the problem of the New England Oil Company tanker which lies stranded and abandoned by her crew on Seal Rock, off Newport. As a result of the conference Major Peterson returned to Rhode Island tonight armed with the War Department's permission to take such action as he may deem best to remove the menace of this oil cargo which is daily becoming more serious.

Before leaving Washington, Major Peterson indicated that the oil tanker has been abandoned by her crew, her owners, and the American Underwriters and all that remains to be done is to secure the abandonment of the British Underwriters which has been cabled for, before he can take action to dispose of the vessel and her cargo . . .

It is pointed out that not only is the oil that is seeping from the tanker through the pasted seams injuring property along the waterfront but that the film of oil is covering the water and the waterfront structures in the vicinity is a potential fire hazard which at any moment may become real. As soon as notice is received from the London Underwriters representative Burdick has been advised steps will be taken to abate the nuisance with as little inconvenience to property owners as possible. Several contractors have looked the vessel over and have given it as their opinion that the cargo cannot be salvaged. The temperature of the water, it is said, is too low to permit of pumping the oil which becomes sluggish at low temperatures and an effort may be made to burn it although the belief has been expressed that this method may not be practicable. The War Department is very anxious to have the oil disposed of with as little delay as possible and no time will be lost by Major Peterson in dealing with the matter when final abandonment of the tanker has been consented to by all parties.

• • •

Newport Daily News: April 30, 1924

OFFICIALS VISIT TANKER
Critical Survey Being Made Of Wreck And Contents Of Tank
Matter Discussed At Meeting Yesterday
And Cooperation From Various Sources Assured

Mayor Sullivan, Major Peterson, and members of the State Board of Purification of Waters, left for the wrecked oil tanker this morning on fishing steamer W. A. Wells and early this afternoon appeared to be a wrecking steamer which came from the westward and for hours men were observed about the wreck. . . . it is inferred that a critical survey was being made of the wreck and the contents of the tanks. As a result the experts will be supplied with an intimate acquaintance of affairs on the ship and it is hoped that through this acquaintance they will find some solution to the problem, namely, to prevent more of the oil from coming ashore. Having gone west nearly to Point Judith and east to Seaconnet and today being found far up the bay, the oil released seems to be of the most broadcasting nature. . . .

The probelm of securing the oil remaining in the vessel and getting rid of the oil already floated ashore is still unsolved. "It's oil, but it won't burn," is the verdict of many and it is reported that a test with gasoline to fuse it has failed totally. Where it has hit beaches some of it forms a plastic mass at the high water mark while below it works into the sand and rolls up into loaves which bury themselves several inches below the surface to be later washed up again. It has been suggested that only blow torches will take it from the rocks. It is because of the damage already done by a small amount of the vessel's cargo that some people are becoming very much concerned lest the ship may have to be blown up, and the oil released all at one time.

• • •

According to the guardsmen, who are watching the ship, there are now signs of her sides cracking open because one end is firmly supported and the other floats in the water.

Newport Daily News: May 1, 1924

PROBLEM UNSOLVED
Thorough Inspection Made of Stranded Oil Tanker
Several Suggestions Offered But
Each Seems To Be Attended by Difficulties

The experts, who visited the stranded tanker yesterday, returned without finding a solution of the problem as to how to abate what may be a further nuisance without further defiling the shores and waters of Rhode Island. The experts said that the oil cannot be pumped out because it is congealed in the tanks and there is no way of heating it with the ship flooded with sea water. To burn it, they feel, threatens more dangers. The tanks are, in reality, compartments in the ship and fire in the oil may be expected to break the bulkheads down allowing seawater to rush in and put out the fire and then the oil will be at liberty to contaminate the sea again.

A most thorough inspection was made of the craft and it was estimated that five-eighths of the ship's cargo, when she struck the ledge, is still in her and will remain there during calm seas, but storm waves breaking over her is sure to send more adrift. One solution of the problem was suggested and that is to cut the section where most of the oil is, float it off the rocks and take it into port where it can be worked upon. This would be an undertaking threatened by many difficulties and may not be decided to be practicable. Considerable water was found to exist all about where the ship rests . . .

• • •

While up to date the coastguardsmen have heard nor seen no signals of distress from the stranded tanker, cries of distress as a result of her stranding are multiplying. Bailey's Beach is ruined, Narragansett Pier Beach is threatened and the fishing rocks off Beavertail are covered.

It is being looked upon as rather strange that a marine catastrophe so quiet at the time has since stirred up so much. A fact not generally known is that Chief Boatswain's Mate Fitzsimmons was in a quandry when the guardsman in the watch tower reported to him that a tanker had come to a stop and lowered boats, but made no signals of any kind. Unable to determine anything from shore, the tanker being without radio, and no signalman appearing to be on duty on her, the acting Captain of the Coast Guard station decided to take a chance and run out quietly and see if there was any trouble. So quietly did he get away that it has been a problem to understand how it was that shortly after the life crew shoved off, the Daily News representative arrived on the scene.

• • •

Newport Daily News: May 2, 1924

TO BURN OIL IN TANKER
Attempt Made This Morning But Heavy Sea Interferes
Further Contamination Of Shores
Prompts Major Peterson To Start Action At Once

After repeated consultations and a thorough weighing of all the propositions advanced, Major Peterson, U.S. Engineer Corps., who was charged by the government with trying to deal with the oil menace from the stranded tanker Llewellyn Howland decided that the time had come for action and so he this morning headed an expedition which went out to Brenton's Reef in the Engineers' boat Monomoy.

On the boat there was a large amount of gasoline in five-gallon tins for ready handling, quantities of burlap, fuse and ropes and an augmented crew. Of all the plans that had been suggested burning seemed to be the most feasible and this was what was attempted. The heavy seas of yesterday and last night have swung the steamer still more and have further racked her so that considerable fresh oil is floating shoreward under the influence of the continuing southwest wind.

. . . . As the Monomoy made out past Brenton's Point it became more and more evident that nothing could be done today but Major Peterson would not give up until Captain Lewis of the Seaconnet Fisheries Company, who was coming in on the steamer Wells, could be interviewed. He said that it would be impossible to board the tanker in such a sea, not even with the aid of his hardy crew of fishermen. . . .

Yesterday Major Peterson made experiments in the burning of a pail of the oil and as he explained the results this morning the situation is not the most encouraging. He learned some things about the non-inflammability of fuel oil under conditions which have to be met on board the tanker and it is hoped the experiments will prove of value when the work is undertaken. He apparently has no idea in mind that even a successful burning will save the shores from at least some further damage for it cannot all be burned but he does, however, feel strongly that an effort to do something must be made at once and that it is better for the whole nuisance to come at once than have the oil seep out of the wreck during the summer. If the source of nuisance can be removed now he feels that the problem of cleaning up the shores and the beaches can be undertaken and that every storm will not cause a fresh contamination of the shores.

The oil is already spread out over a wide area it having been reported off Clay Head, Block Island and threatening invasion of Long Island Sound.

The ideal conditions for the burning of oil would be a good northwesterly breeze not only to flatten down the sea but to take the smoke and the floating oil far out to sea.

Newport Daily News: May 3, 1924

FIRE STARTED ON OIL TANKER THIS MORNING
Blaze Will Continue For At Least Forty-Eight Hours
Making A Fine Night Spectacular

The stranded tanker Llewellyn Howland with her cargo of fuel oil successfully fired this morning by U.S. Army Engineer Forces under the direction of Major Peterson in charge of this district and the burning ship should be a spectacular sight from the Ocean Drive this evening and perhaps tomorrow evening.

The firing went off strictly according to plans but none of the horrible things which some people feared materialized and the Newport firemen who were sent with their apparatus to the shore had little more to do than look on.

• • •

Shortly before 9 o'clock the party boarded the tanker and began operations. For better than an hour they tore down partitions in the bow, gathered mattresses and everything else and threw them into the five tanks. Fuses were then trimmed and gasoline poured into the five tanks. At 10:10 orders were given to the Monomoy to stand by and all but two men were taken off and placed on board the government steamer. Of the two men left on board one was Mr. Smith of the New England Oil Company who was honored with being selected to set it off.

Hanging by a rope at the bow, Mr. Smith reached through a porthole and ignited a fuse and then dropped into a longboat rolling and pitching alongside and the fishermen rowed to the Monomoy which laid off a little distance while those on board watched the minutes roll off. It was figured that the fuse would burn ten minutes but burned a little longer. Then came a flash from the gunpowder which was the first sign to the anxious ones that the fuse had done its work. Soon there was another flash and that announced that the rope fuse had fired tank number one and then at intervals there were flashes as each side of the four additional tanks caught.

• • •

The little puffs and streaks of smoke gradually increased as the oil heated up and began vaporizing until about 12:30 the cloud of smoke making a spectacle but what the close observers noted with gratification was that the heat on board had become so intense that it was passing through the bunkers and blistering the paint on the side of the ship. The firing force then headed for the harbor. It was calculated that within a few hours the wooden deck would burn off and this would give more vent to the flames and cause them to burn more furiously hence it is felt that tonight will offer a grand spectacle of a ship on fire at sea with flames leaping into the air.

Since only the upper surface of the oil in the tanks can burn, it is calculated by the various oil men who went out that it will take perhaps two full days for the oil to burn itself out which it will do it is believed unless there should come up a storm which would raise the seas so that they will drown out the flames.

• • •

Newport Daily News: May 5, 1924

OIL STILL BURNING

Fire On Tanker Shows No Signs Of Going Out
Drive Crowded Saturday And Sunday
With Cars From Massachusetts And This State

The firing of the oil on the stranded tanker Saturday was no haphazard undertaking but one which had been carefully worked out by Major Peterson with the advice of experts of the Standard and New England Oil Companies. . . .

One thing that was positive was that a temperature of upwards of one hundred and ninety degrees must be obtained to ignite the oil. This meant that no minor blaze could set it off and that it would be necessary to generate huge heat in the tanks hence elaborate priming preparations. The real fire was slow in developing for the reason that at first it was only the priming that burned and it took time for the oil itself to warm up and then the firing party had no tears except that the terrible heat might melt down the sides of the ship to where the ocean swells could flow in or there might arise a storm which could cause seas which would flood the ship. . . .

From the spectacular point of view there has been disappointment for those with elaborate imaginations because the oil did not float out and fingers of fire were not stretching out in various directions threatening shipping and perhaps the rocky coast . . . Yesterday the sides were white showing the intense heat within but the constant wash of the sea kept the sides from melting down.

It was anticipated that a few hours after the fire had got underway that the deck would burn off and then with greater vent the fire would burn with greater intensity. This has occurred. It was anticipated also that the iron walls between the tanks would melt down and make the tanks one. This is presumed to have taken place but the heat is so intense that no one has been able to approach close enough to assure themselves of this fact.

• • •

The oil which wouldn't burn is burning and at present shows no sign of going out though the forty-eight hours which it was estimated would be required to burn out the tanker have passed. The Llewellyn Howland has now lost her bridge house which went Saturday night and she looks just what she is a torn and wrent piece of junk just at present still containing fuel.

It is hoped that the fire will end any further possibilities of damaging the shores by oil but still there are some unknown quantities for the after part of the ship has been submerged since she was abandoned and it is not known just what oil remains there while no one can tell how thoroughly the fire will burn the oil forward as there may come a drowning out before the fire completes its work.

• • •

All the thrills expected from a spectacle of a ship on fire at sea were realized near midnight Sunday when the wind died down and the sea became calm as the oil on the tanker burned brightly causing a reflection in the water and throwing a radiance over several miles as the burning of the oil progressed to its ultimate conclusion. The sight was one which caused several thousand automobiles to come from other cities and traffic officers reported that no day in mid-summer found more machines coming into the city.

The spectacular blaze continued for several days before finally burning out and leaving a charred hulk on the ledge. In contrast to the journalistic style of the Daily News reporter we have the succinct and detailed report of the Corps of Engineers which is offered to the reader as an illustration of the amount of technical information not offered by the newspaper but still of interest to the interested wreck searcher.

The following report is submitted of operations in connection with the burning of the oil cargo in the tanker LLEWELLYN HOW-LAND, reference being made to letter of Chief of Engineers dated May 28, 1924, file 7120 (LLEWELLYN HOWLAND).

1. On April 21, 1924, about 11:00 A.M., tank steamer Llewellyn Howland, en route from Fall River, Mass. to Portland, Me., with a cargo of 25,000 barrels of fuel oil, ran hard aground upon Seal Ledge, a mile off the southerly shore of Newport, R.I., near the entrance to Narragansett Bay. Her crew was rescued without difficulty by the U.S. Coast Guard from Price's Neck Station, about 1¼ miles distant. The vessel became a total wreck during the southerly gale which began that afternoon and continued for two days. Although at first headed in an easterly direction, in her final position after the storm subsided her bow pointed off shore or almost due south (magnetic).

2. The vessel was making her maiden voyage under the name Llewellyn Howland, her previous name having been the WICO. Originally she was the German tank steamer PAULA, built in 1888 at Low Walker-on-Tyne, England. Her registered dimensions are: length 283.1 feet; breadth 40.3 feet; depth 30.3 feet; tonnage 2,748 gross tons and 1,715 net; indicated horsepower 1,250.

3. During the gale and for several days afterward, large quantities of

thick oil came from the vessel and were deposited on the neighboring shores, particularly the beaches and rocks around Newport, where it became a very serious detriment not only to the beautiful shore estates but to the entire city as a popular summer resort. Masses of oil were also reported to be floating in considerable quantities near Block Island, over 15 miles away, and to have come ashore on Rhode Island beaches more than 20 miles west from the wreck.

4. Urgent appeals by the city of Newport and influential property owners for early action to supress this menace were at once made to the owners of the cargo, and to State and United States authorities. After conferences between the interested parties, including owners, underwriters, and representatives of the city, state and United States, the District Engineer was summoned to Washington for consultation with the Chief of Engineers and the Secretary of War on April 28th. As a result, the task of removing the oil from the vessel as soon as possible was assigned to the District Engineer on the ground that it was a menace to navigation, since shipping would be endangered if any of the floating oil became ignited.

5. Thereupon, it became a question of the best method to pursue to accomplish this object. Since there was no known precedent to follow, further conferences among the local interests were held, not only for the purpose of discussing feasible methods of procedure, but also to keep these interests and the public fully informed as to the difficulties of the work and the progress being made toward the solution of the problem.

6. On April 30th, an inspection of the vessel by the District Engineer, accompanied by the Mayor and other officials of Newport, representatives of the State Legislature and State Board of Purification of Waters, representatives of the New England Oil Company and the Standard Oil Company, and wrecking experts from the Merritt-Chapman & Scott Corporation disclosed the following facts: That the vessel was fast on the ledge and showed a slight break across her iron hull just forward of the midship deckhouse and navigating bridge; that the bottom of the vessel was badly punctured; that her main deck at the stern was about awash at low water, while at the forward mast the deck was approximately three feet above high tide, the range of tide being 3.5 feet; that the hull had a slight list to starboard; that it was impossible to remove the vessel as a whole without an enormous expenditure of money unwarranted by the conditions and requiring much time; that approximately 16,000 barrels of thick oil remained in the 16 tanks, these being arranged in 8 pairs, viz.: 2 pairs forward of the mast, 4 pairs between the forward mast and midship deckhouse, 1 pair under and 1 pair just aft of the midship deckhouse, the after end of the rear pair being forward of the smokestack; that the oil was too thick to be pumped without first heating it approximately fifty degrees; and that small patches of thick oil were coming from the vessel almost continually.

7. Consideration was given to the suggestion of pumping the

remaining oil from the tanks but the estimated amount of heat required to raise the temperature of the oil sufficiently to permit pumping it was greater than could be supplied by any feasible method, since it was impracticable to install a heating plant on the vessel owing to the heavy seas that were prevailing from time to time, and also impossible to keep a lighter alongside the wreck except during occasional short intervals when the sea was smooth. Furthermore, if the oil could be made liquid enough for pumping, the operation of pumping would be hazardous owing to the usual daily winds and rough water.

8. Experiments with samples taken from the tanker indicated that the oil could be burned if once ignited by the aid of a highly combustible fuel, such as gasoline. Accordingly, it was decided, on May 1st, to set fire to as many tanks as possible as soon as favorable weather conditions permitted. The equipment was assembled early May 2nd, but the wind and seas proved too high to chance boarding the wreck that day. At 9 A.M., May 3rd although the sea was far from calm, the equipment and a working force of 12 men, under the personal direction of the District Engineer, and also experts from the two oil companies, were transferred from the Engineer Department survey cruiser MONOMOY to the forward deck of the HOWLAND with the aid of a rugged seine boat and the work of rigging up for the burning was immediately commenced.

9. Hatch covers on the 3 pairs of tanks farthest forward were first opened up and lashed back with chains found on board. These covers were of heavy iron, about 5 feet long by 4 feet wide, and hinged along the midship side, so that when open the two in each pair stood back to back and in a favorable position for lashing together. While this work was in progress and wood for fuel was being obtained by tearing down the partitions, closets, etc. in the forward quarters, the placing of the lighting contrivance was being carried on. Wicks of old ¾″ diameter rope, wrapped spirally with burlap tied loosely at about 3 feet intervals, were strung longitudinally over the hatches in two lines, one over the port hatches and the other over the starboard, with two leaders branching into each tank and hanging down to the surface of the oil. At the lower end of each leader a loose bundle of burlap was attached to give volume to the ignition flame when it reached the oil. The wicks were wired to hatch railings and other convenient objects to secure them against possible displacement, and the forward ends of the two longitudinals were brought into a junction box containing a flash pan located on the main deck forward of the forward pair of tanks and under an overhang of the upper deck in the bow. This box was a common grocery box about ⅔ the size of an egg case, and the flash pan was a small cooking tin in which was placed half a pound of gunpowder. Around the pan box was filled loosely with excelsior, obtained from some of the ship's mattresses, to transmit the flame from the powder to the wicks. From the powder, about 30 feet of ordinary blasting fuse, having a known burning rate of 2 feet per minute, was run to a hawser-hole in the port bow of the vessel. To provide against

possible failure in igniting the wicks if the fuse happened to be defective, another junction box with separate flash pan, powder and fuse was arranged near the second pair of tanks with branch wicks leading from it to both longitudinal wicks. The hatches of two more pairs of tanks, the 4th and 5th from the bow, were opened as soon as the tide fell and the seas ceased to wash over them. These were prepared for igniting by extending the two longitudinal wicks over them and running leaders into them the same as described above for the other tanks farther forward. All available wood, excelsior and surplus burlap and wicking was then thrown into these ten tanks, and lastly, 230 gallons of gasoline were poured in, about 23 gallons per tank, while 10 gallons were used to saturate the wicks and 10 gallons were poured on the wooden deck on the port side of the ship between the iron neck of the tanks and the hull.

10. Immediately after the gasoline was distributed, all hands except two were transferred to the MONOMOY, which had been lying to nearby. Igniting the fuses from the outside of the hull was attended by some danger on account of the rough sea making it impossible to hold the small boat alongside. The fuse lighting was finally accomplished by using a rope looped over the side of the vessel to provide footing for a man while applying the match. Both the remaining men then jumped into the small boat which was rowed away rapidly and taken in tow by the MONOMOY to a safe distance to the windward.

11. It was 11:10 A.M. when the fuses were lighted and in 14 minutes the powder flash in the forward junction box was seen, followed in less than two minutes by a similar flash in the other flash box. The flame was soon observed travelling slowly along the longitudinal rope wicks from hatch to hatch. Beginning in the forward tanks and progressing successively in the tanks aft, light smoke gradually issued in increasing volumes for about an hour, when it was evident from the change to heavy black smoke that the oil in all the 5 pairs of tanks prepared for lighting was actually burning and the plans as conceived were proving successful.

12. The fire burned continuously until 11:15 P.M. on May 8th or a little more than 130 hours. Its intensity and extent throughout the ship varied more or less from time to time. At first, it was mostly confined to the 3 or 4 pairs of forward tanks, but after 48 hours, when the sea became nearly calm, it spread to the tanks aft of those originally lighted and at low tide all the tanks were burning fiercely. Gradually the plates of the forward part of hull became warped and vertical splits appeared in both sides nearly opposite the foremast, extending down below the water level, allowing some of the heated oil to flow out. Occasionally small patches of this oil coming out would burn while close to the intense heat near the ship, and one night the Coast Guard claimed to have seen some burning about ¼ mile away, although no one else has been found to confirm this statement. It is thought that possibly the spectacle was caused by a reflection on the water from the blazing oil in or close to the vessel. From the third to the fifth days, the fire was at its

The author with the first of two cannon retrieved from the Spanish Brig *Minerva* by a team of divers that consisted of himself and Navy Chief Torpedoman Jon Hentz. *Photo from the author's collection.*

Transparent treasure—old glass. Photo from the author's collection.

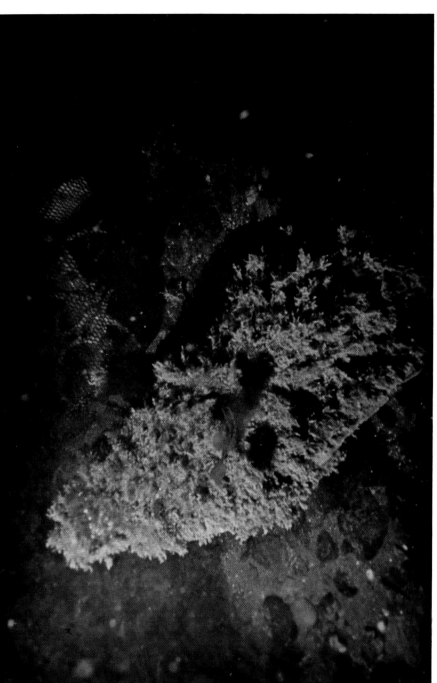

Camouflage is readily attracted to shipwreck material, very often making objects difficult to identify. Pictured is the fluke of an anchor that has lain on the sea floor for probably seventy years. *Photo from the author's collection.*

An intact porthole and rim from the sidewheel steamer *Rhode Island. Photo from the author's collection.*

It can be seen easily why the ship's wheel is one of the most sought after trophies of every ambitious wreck diver. *Photo from the author's collection.*

A ship's propeller weighing approximately one hundred pounds. *Photo from the author's collection.*

The tanker *Llewellyn Howland* as it appears today—more than fifty years after her loss. Her plates, twisted and scattered, have become a picturesque haven for local inhabitants. *Photo from the author's collection.*

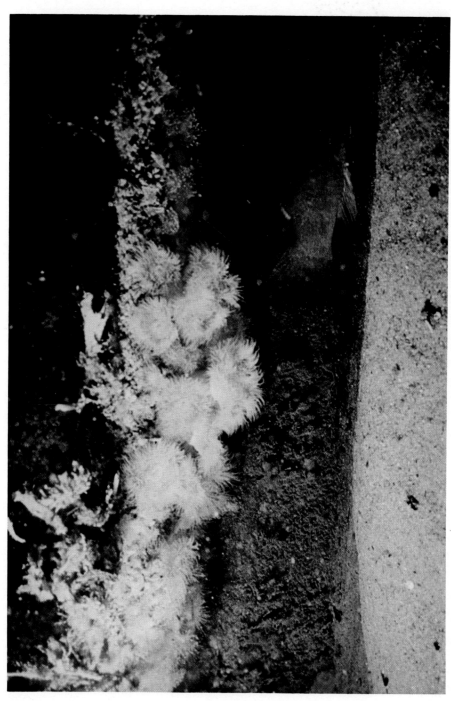

Despite the intactness of the remains of the *Hilda Garston*, the limitations of visibility prevent good distance shots of the vessel. Shown here is the sandy bottom that surrounds, supports, and may eventually swallow the wreck.

greatest height, and all woodwork above low water was entirely consumed, except the roof of the stern deckhouse. The interior ironwork forward of the stack was buckled and twisted, and the bridge extending forward from the midship house supported by iron columns was completely destroyed. On the fifth day, after 120 hours of burning, the fire decreased rapidly and died out entirely at about high water, 10 hours later, the sea at that time being somewhat rough from the strong northeast wind that had been blowing during the afternoon and evening.

13. An examination of the wreck from the deck of the MONOMOY after the burning showed considerable thick tarry residue confined within the vessel between the upper portion of the forward tanks and the sides of the hull. This adhered more or less to the ironwork, but most of it floated on the water surface as the tide rose and fell. Occasionally, small masses oozed out through narrow openings in the hull plates, or were washed out by the heavy seas, and drifted away.

14. For several days it was too rough to permit boarding the wreck and making a close inspection of the tanks to ascertain how much oil and residue remained in them. At low water on May 16th, however, this was done and revealed the following conditions:

Assigning numbers to pairs of tanks in order of their position, beginning with #1 the farthest forward and ending with #8 the farthest aft:—

#1 and #2 contained about 6″ of oily residue.

#3 had no oil, the sides of the upper portion being broken, allowing the contents to spread.

#4 and #5 contained about 2 feet of oily residue; port side of the upper portion of #4 port tank was split, but oil to thick to escape.

#6 contained about 3 feet of very thick oily residue of a consistency similar to thin putty; side walls split through where hull was originally broken; contents too thick to escape.

#7 contained about 3 feet of thick oil and residue; hatch cover on starboard tank bent open slightly.

#8 contained about 18″ of oil and residue, medium thick; hatch cover on starboard tank bent over slightly.

All ironwork inside the hull above low water was covered with 1″ to 3″ of thick sticky residue like soft tar; this being apparently some of the mass confined within the forward part of the hull which had been spread about by heavy seas. It was roughly estimated that not more than 500 barrels of oil and residue remained in the vessel. Although this was only a relatively small quantity and was coming away from the wreck very gradually, the public demands for complete removal of the "oil menace" made it extremely desirable that the remainder of the cargo be released at once.

15. As a first step toward this end, hatch covers on the three after tanks, #6, #7, and #8, were removed in order to allow their contents to be churned out as much as possible during high water and heavy

seas. For the other tanks, particularly numbers 4 and 5, and to release the mess confined within the sides of the forward portion of the hull, it was decided that explosive charges would be required. To expedite this work, conferences were held with the Inspector of Ordnance in Charge of the Naval Torpedo Station, at Newport, R.I., where submarine explosives are manufactured, and it was arranged that depth charges be prepared at the station and that the station forces handle, place, and fire them.

16. On May 21st, the assembling of the material was completed. Next morning, under favorable weather conditions and at high tide, two 300-lb. charges of TNT were placed in the tanks about 10 feet below the surface of the semi-liquid oil, one in the after part of #6 port tank and one in the forward part of #5 starboard tank. At 11:50 A.M., May 22nd, these were fired by a 25 dry cell battery on a lighter anchored about 2,000 feet away. A huge column of water, with oil and pieces of iron, rose approximately 150 feet in the air, followed by a series of loud reports made by the falling iron on the deck of the tanker and adjacent waters. The dislodged oil and residue was broken up into a thick, soupy condition and covered an area approximately 100 feet by 200 feet as it drifted away in an offshore direction. All tanks were opened and a wide opening across the hull was made about amidships; the midship deckhouse was demolished and both masts were broken off; large pieces of the iron plating were thrown and torn out of place and left an irregular mass of debris. Oil practically ceased coming from the wreck within a few hours, the only oil visible thereafter being that attached to the mass of ironwork.

17. During the following few days of rough weather, the after part of the wreck broke apart, the midship deckhouse and the after deckhouse disappeared, and the stern settled down out of sight at low water, leaving visible above water only the smokestack with a small section of the deck near it, and the bow portion of the hull still intact. These conditions were observed May 27th and have remained the same since.

18. A day or two after the tanks were blown up, a gas buoy was placed outside the wreck by the Lighthouse Department approximately in the position of buoy N2, shown on U.S. Coast & Geodetic Survey Chart 353. This was done without consulting this office and no official communication has been received regarding it.

19. The wreck is now resting firmly in 26 to 32 feet of water on the westerly portion of Seal Ledge, about 500 feet southwest of the shoalest spot on which there is but 17 feet, and 500 feet northwest of the southerly tip on which there is 23 feet. The location is about 300 feet inside the buoy marking the safe limits for deep draft vessels, and the ½ mile of trecherous water inside extending nearly to Seal Rock is unused except by small fishing boats operated during daylight hours. In view of these conditions, together with the probability that the existing portions of the hull will not break up for at least several months, it is recommended that no action toward removing the remainder of the wreck be taken at present, but that decision as to the

final disposition of the hull be postponed until there are indications of disintegration.

20. Occasional inspections will be made to observe such changes as may occur and to furnish a basis for later considerations of the matter.

21. It may be pertinent to add that the Commandant of the Naval Station at Newport, with whom the subject of removal has been discussed verbally, concurs in the recommendations above.

V. L. Peterson
Major, Corps of Engineers

After reading these reports it was impossible to pass up the chance to search for so valiant a ship which had withstood the trials of wind, water, and fire. Accordingly, we made plans to search the sea to the westward of Seal Ledge and see for ourselves how much remained of this ship after almost fifty years in the sea.

DIVE #1, Year 1, May 9th—Anchoring in the approximate location described in the Engineer's Report we began our search today for the remains of the oil tanker *Llewellyn Howland*. We decided a preliminary free swimming search was called for to determine the exact bottom topography and as this was a fairly well documented wreck we even had hopes of an instant find. These hopes were not completely realized but we did manage to locate a very large anchor chain which must surely belong to the tanker as no other wrecks of considerable size to warrant such a large chain had occurred in the vicinity.

DIVE #2, July 18th—After searching for awhile we came across the anchor chain previously located but we were unable to trace it back to the wreck as we had hoped. We have reason to suspect that the wreck lies near the western extremity of this chain but out diving time here has been somewhat limited because of our other wreck interests which are currently keeping us quite busy. *(Note: Although we had read the newspaper accounts of the disaster we did not acquire the Engineers' Report until much later, hence the reference to thinking that the wreck would lie at the western extremity of the chain.)*

DIVE #3, Year 2, May 29th—We used the fathometer to pinpoint Seal Ledge as we have found buoy #2 moves slightly from time to time and after almost an hour of searching at the western end of the chain we discovered an area of major wreckage. As we were out of air we could do no more than to take land ranges on this location which we plan to revisit soon.

DIVE #4, June 5th—After spending considerable time in the area of

our somewhat inaccurate land ranges our efforts were rewarded hand-
somely. Before our eyes lay the living proof of the story we had read of a
ship twisted and rent by the forces of the sea and the immense fire.
Distinguishable among these objects were the boiler, an immense winch,
two bollards or bitts (by which a ship is tied to a pier or wharf), and
numerous iron plates scattered about like a deck of cards. On the one
hand, we were ecstatic at finding the wreck after only three dives but, on
the other hand, the wreck, although in almost forty feet of water, was
considerably broken up.

DIVE #5, June 17th—We decided that this site would be best studied
with the use of an underwater sled. Our composite map of the area was
started and we knew that a trip across the wreck with the sled would help
us pinpoint the relationship of one object to another with much greater
ease than we would otherwise have. The sledding venture revealed to us
that our composite was already quite complete. This was a fascinating
dive indeed and we noted with great pleasure that there were many fine
artifacts in this area.

DIVE #6, October 2nd—Today we encountered a severe surge on the
wreck. Although we had noted a constant surge on our previous dives it
had not been to the extent that we now experienced. From the pockets of
tarry residue still remaining here after almost fifty years I retrieved what
has to be the indicator arm from the ship's telegraph. Apparently the
remains are lying bow to southward but considerably spread out. The
surge makes the diving here somewhat difficult and artifact retrieval a
difficult job but nonetheless today's dive saw a porthole rim come to the
surface to spend its final days as a display on a wreck searcher's wall.

DIVE #7, Year 3, May 14th—The *Llewellyn Howland* has now
become a backup dive for our wreck searching activities in the surrounding area. The decision to make this wreck a backup dive for further
searching activities came only after we made an attempt to physically grid
this site as a project for our team. Due to the incessant surge in the area we
found it next to impossible to lay out a grid or even to use a compass with
any efficiency. A free swimming diver here is simply at the mercy of the
surge. However, since the site is still a good one to dive and many of our
divers regard it as the best of our "near at hand" wrecks, we decided to
visit this wreck at least twice annually to continue to add to the
completion of our composite map of this wrecksite. In addition to the
objects mentioned before as being located today we have added to our
composite map an air ventilator, two large anchors, numerous porthole
rims (which we have left for future wreck searchers to find and retrieve),
and two square cement blocks each approximately four feet square and

deep and joined by a length of heavy chain about twenty five feet long. This last object puzzles us and our best guess is that it served as some sort of mooring for a vessel which may have at some time worked in this area on the remains of the tanker. Research has not turned up any such vessel or operation but between 1924 and the present there have been a lot of newspaper reports to be studied which may yet reveal just such an operation.

Since this time we have visited the remains of the *Llewellyn Howland* over a dozen times and even now we are bringing to light new artifacts, mainly of a non-ferrous nature, as new divers in our team have the opportunity to see this wreck for the first time.

We have located several other large modern vessels in this depth of water and have found most to be in about this condition thus prompting us to go just a little deeper to locate the optimum in intact wrecks. Such was the case with the fishing vessel *Hilda Garston* which was lost in 1961 off the nearby Massachusetts coast.

8 *Hilda Garston*

S EVERAL times in recent years an elusive or exceptional wreck has teased the fancy of our divers and led to a very interesting search as we enjoyed when searching for the steel fishing dragger *Hilda Garston*. The background material on this wreck was brief and a little mysterious. Returning from a successful voyage, her hold filled with scallops, the *Hilda Garston* cruised toward New Bedford, Massachusetts on a cold and dreary night in February of 1961. Without warning she struck some unknown object and immediately began to fill with water as her weary crew made their way to her dories. There was time enough only to send a distress call to the Coast Guard and board the dories before the vessel went to the bottom. The crew made it to shore in safety and within a day or two the owners made plans to locate and raise the vessel, if possible. After several harrowing experiences by the salvagers all attempts to salvage the vessel were abandoned and, thus, the *Hilda Garston* became yet another in the long list of vessels to join New England's sunken fleet.

Our interest in the *Hilda Garston* came about for two reasons—both rumors. The first was that the ship was said to be nearly intact and upright on the bottom. The second reason was that the divers involved with her salvage were reportedly unable to relocate her remains when choosing to do so for a fun dive. She was beginning to gain a reputation as a wandering shipwreck and this challenge brought our interest to a peak rapidly. For several weeks we discussed the possibility of making a trip to the general area of the wreck to see if we could have any better luck in locating her. With such a monumental task ahead of us we were ready to give it a try with as many boats and divers as we could employ.

The dawn on the day of our search was bright and clear and the water calm. Three boats and seven divers would be available for our search in hopes that we could cover as much territory as possible in the shortest period of time. The chart of the area was marked with the approximate position of our quarry and the remains were supposedly only twelve feet below the surface in fifty eight feet of water. Team #1 consisted of my diving partner and myself, and, since our boat was the only one with a fathometer, our job was to leave for the site two hours ahead of the other boats and try to locate the wreck using just the fathometer. If that method failed we would run the three boats on a parallel course with each towing a diver on a sled.

After about an hour on the water Team #1 arrived at the site at 7:00 A.M. to begin the search. The Coast Guard had long since marked the area with an obstruction buoy but our faith in buoys which can drift off station has been very poor since the first time we made the mistake of using a buoy as part of a land range and found out just how much difference even the change in tide can make in returning to the same spot. Our first run in the area was begun with the assumption that the buoy was in its proper location. This course turned up no results and neither did the second nor third runs. After about an hour and about seven compass runs using the fathometer we decided that something was wrong here, indeed. Checking with the chart (Coast & Geodetic Survey Chart #237) we determined that there were three rockpiles on the ocean side of the buoy that would come up off the bottom enough to give us a reading. If these were in their proper positions in relation to the buoy then the buoy should be in the correct spot. If not, we could search for the wreck from these rockpiles if we could locate them. This seemed like the logical direction to proceed and was quickly agreed upon. In short order we located each of the rockpiles and decided that the buoy was, indeed, located where it should be. Why no wreck?

We crisscrossed the area several more times with the same results and then decided to try another location just east of the area where the wreck should lie. No results again and no hopeful signs either. It was nearing 9:00 A.M. now and we spotted one of the other boats from our team on its way out to our location. We were disappointed that we hadn't located and buoyed the wreck by this time but we knew with the approach of our other divers would come a fresh enthusiasm to bolster our spirits for the long task that was to come.

With the arrival of the other boats we quickly discussed our lack of success so far and decided to put our divers in the water immediately and begin the sledding operation. As we were using only planing boards with no communication systems, each diver would be required to tow a small buoy so that his dropping off the sled would not go unnoticed. Each of the three divers chosen to sled began to "suit up" and as we watched hopefully they entered the water. Every diver on the team silently wished that he might be the one to first sight the wreck and the competitive nature of the team members did much to bolster the moral of the team in general.

As I watched, my diving partner descended into the eerie gloom of the water and quickly settled himself on the bottom giving me the three tugs on the line necessary before I would get underway. Flanked by one boat on each side at fifty foot intervals I started the outboard motor, checked the gas and the compass, and headed out from the arbitrarily chosen starting point in the direction of shore. Glancing over my shoulder I noticed that the buoy to be towed by my sledding partner was not moving. As he had given me the three tugs on the bridle of the sled indicating that he was ready to go I could only assume that he had somehow lost his buoy line and did not know it. In most cases this would mean a restart but since I knew he had his inflatable buoy and line with him I chose to continue rather than upset the search pattern we had set up. After running about one quarter mile we were ready to come about and begin the second leg of our search. I decided to retrieve my partner first and return for the lost buoy in the boat but as I pulled in the underwater sled it proved to be unoccupied. I was not sure whether to be happy or scared because the empty sled meant one of two things: 1) my partner had found the wreck of Hilda already or 2) he was in trouble! Very little time was lost in speeding back to the starting point where the buoy was still floating idly on the surface of the water. As anxious moments dragged by I awaited my companion's return to the surface. Suddenly he was there with a huge smile on his face asking for the anchor so that he could hook it in the wreck. I could hardly believe my ears. I had dropped him ten feet from the deck of the *Hilda Garston!*

Being used to long hard days of searching, many of which have been unsuccessful, the thought of such a rapid success was unbelievable. In short order, however, the entire crew of divers were dressed and began entering the water to catch a first glimpse of our newest wreck. My partner had stayed on the surface just long enough to get his tools and to tell me that the wreck was, indeed, intact. In only moments I would have the opportunity to see just how fine a prize we had found.

Descending, at last, my thoughts wandered to the sight that would appear through the gloom but I was hardly prepared for what soon fell within my limited vision. The scene before me was like any scuba diver's wildest dream. The *Hilda Garston* was sitting here on a sandy bottom in a seemingly undamaged condition. Our anchor was attached at the bow and the scene looking aft was spectacular. Swimming along the deck our divers noticed small debris lying here and there scattered about as if a small tornado had struck leaving piles of iron and other objects deposited at several points on the deck. The wind cover over the forward ladder to the forecastle was intact and passing it we noticed a large winch on the starboard side. As we poked around the deck, still moving toward the stern, we were suddenly faced with the pilothouse which rose off the level of the deck a full twelve feet. It was simply fantastic to peer through the barren holes, which once held the windows of the pilothouse, into the emptiness within. Even the walkway around the pilothouse, complete with railing, was intact and in seemingly perfect order. We swam around the pilothouse to the small section of deck behind it and over the stern railing to the sandy bottom. It was just about a perfect shipwreck. Entering the cabin just aft of the pilothouse we faced an inky blackness within until, flashing on our underwater lights, the innermost portions of the ship revealed themselves to us. Along the bulkheads at evenly spaced intervals were portholes, some still with intact glass, and our eyes grew wide at the promise of a good artifact for each of us. The cabin deck was somewhat strewn with debris as the deck had been but there was more than enough room for all of us to maneuver with ease. It was only a short swim through the cabin to the ladder which brought us up into the pilothouse where each of us in turn stood a silent moment where the wheel had been and imagined himself as captain of this undersea vessel. Gazing around the pilothouse we noted that all of the electronic equipment essential to the operation of a modern fishing vessel had been removed but even devoid of its normal equipment the pilothouse gave each of our enthusiastic divers the feeling of a happily successful wreck search.

Swimming toward the bow again we passed over two open hatches which obviously led to the cargo holds below. As each of us in turn entered the darkness of this inner room our lights brought life back to this long since unlit area of the ship. The cargo of scallops had long since escaped their confines leaving for us to see a scene of interest to all. As most of our divers had not been within the hold of a fishing vessel before they all took a good long look around. It was simple to see that each one was envisioning the fine treasure to be found just around the next corner.

A glance at my submersible gauge told me that it was time to get to work and find an artifact quickly before my limited air supply would be exhausted. Quickly returning to the cabin below the pilothouse I chose a porthole as a fitting artifact and I moved in close to get a good look at its fastenings. Setting my bag of tools on the deck below I shone my light over the waiting treasure to determine just what tools would be required. Four dogs and a brass dowel fastened with a cotter pin at each end were the only obstacles between me and this fine artifact and it looked like this job would be an easy one. A hammer and a pair of pliers should do the trick but as I glanced through my bag of tools I was utterly dismayed to find that my pliers had been forgotten at the shore. No matter, I could do the job with my hammer and knife. Brass nuts on brass bolts are usually quite a pleasure on a wreck since they do not seize up with rust as iron or steel nuts do. In short order the four dogs which kept the porthole closed in heavy weather were in my bag and the job was already half done. Using my knife blade as a wedge I went to work removing one of the cotter pins in the brass dowel. This was the last obstacle between us. This job proved to be quite time consuming and a glance at my submersible gauge told me that I had but little time left in which to retrieve the prize. Working slowly but diligently the cotter pin was slowly but surely moving and this artifact would soon be mine. With only moments of air left the cotter pin broke and the pieces fell to the deck below. Now I had only the task of driving the brass dowel through the eyes on the porthole rim. I worked very quickly now as I could feel the air becoming harder to pull through my regulator as the supply dwindled. Suddenly it was free and my task was successfully completed. I quickly and gently placed the porthole in my bag and began the trip back to the anchor line at the bow and the return to the surface world above. Rather than try to carry the heavy bag topside I decided to tie the entire bag to the anchor line and haul it into the boat after surfacing and taking off my gear.

Returning to the boat I found the other members of the team awaiting my return. The incessant chatter going on between teammates was readily indicative that all had experienced a fine wreck dive and were thoroughly satisfied with their artifacts. Of the seven divers visiting the wreck, four had retrieved a porthole each, two had retrieved other brass items, and only one diver, my partner, who had been the first diver on the wreck, returned without an artifact. We kidded him to no end over this but he steadfastly maintained that he had been so enthralled with the sight below that he had not even thought about an artifact.

As we were diving almost three miles off shore and we planned to return to the site on the next weekend we decided to leave the wreck buoyed for the present. The remainder of the day was spent in blissful enjoyment as we all soaked up some sun and did some snorkeling at a nearby deserted island. For years to come we will always remember the day that the wandering shipwreck was found by our enthusiastic team of wreck searchers.

Our return dive to the *Hilda Garston* was on a day of fine conditions, even equalling those of the day of first diving there. Most of our divers had brought their tools again but chose to dive without them to study the wreck in greater detail rather than to recover further artifacts. The visibility on this dive was not quite as good as on the former dive but few of our divers cared as long as there was enough visibility for them to sightsee. The goal for most of the divers was the forecastle and other areas forward while others sought only the engine room or a general survey of the entire wreck. On the first dive here I had spotted a ladder from the cabin behind the pilothouse which had to lead directly to the engine room and to this ladder I swam without hesitation. Swimming down a ladder is always a weird sensation to many divers and looking at a room upside down from the ladder is truly a mind-boggling experience. The cramped condition of the engine room was intensified by the huge pile of sand and sediment which covered the entire area of the engine and a short inspection of this portion of the vessel showed that there was little to explore here.

Returning to the pilothouse I decided to swim again through the ship's hold to see if I might spot any missed super goody. There were no other divers in the hold as I entered but the silt within had been much stirred up, limiting visibility to about two feet or less. Picking around the hold I saw nothing of importance here but before leaving I decided to check the overhead and in doing so I discovered one of the finest pieces of wreck treasure that I have ever retrieved from a small wreck. Attached to the beams were a series of brass cage lights which were completely intact even to the light bulbs within. In short order I returned to the boat for my tools and returned to pry off one of these gems for my den. I decided that if time permitted and the air lasted I would retireve two as they would serve as port and starboard lights at my back door. It took a few minutes to determine the best method of retrieval as the wiring for these lights was still in place. I found that by using my hammer as a crowbar and twisting the wires connected to the lamps I was able to pull the electrical connections free at the base of each light and soon had my artifacts safely tucked away in my bag. Leaving my bag at the base of the buoy line I had some time to do some more looking around and soon found one of our other divers struggling with a porthole and, it seemed, apparently losing the battle. He flashed me a glance at his submersible gauge which showed that he had only about a quarter of a tank of air left so I decided to stay and help him retireve his first porthole. In short order he knew just what to do and with very little air left his prize came free of its rim and waving a thank you he sped for the surface with his artifact in hand. Finding ourselves alone on the wreck and completely satisfied with our dive my partner and

I decided to return to the boat and have some lunch. Removing the anchor from the wreck and tying off the tool bags to it we surfaced to enjoy the rest of the day in planning for our next wreck search.

Altogether from the dives that we had made on *Hilda* our seven divers retrieved seven portholes, four brass cage lights, and several other small brass objects. Everyone was happy with his prize. Since the second dive we have revisited the wreck three times and it has become a favorite in the many dives that we have made in that area of coastline. An extensive photographic expedition has been planned but has not been carried out so far as we have found a maximum visibility on our visits here of fifteen feet. There is a medium strength current that runs through the area at certain times but it is not troublesome to those diving within the wreck and can be avoided completely by checking the time of the tides against the coastal pilot for Buzzard's Bay.

Thus, by utilizing the techniques explained in Part I we have been enabled to spend many pleasurable hours researching for and diving on relics of the past and present which have been lost to Neptune's grasp. It must be mentioned here that the opportunity to drop a diver on the deck of a shipwreck involves a great deal of luck. Although the skill required in searching for and locating shipwrecks is involved in every attempt, the factors of good weather and good luck always play a large part in your search. The key word in the physical searching aspect of this sport is persistence. Many days have been spent in search of much larger vessels with very different and less successful results but as your experience increases your odds become much better that you will become a successful wreck searcher and will have many pleasurable hours of wreck diving to look forward to.

Part III

PREFACE

Part II illustrated how our team of divers has utilized the techniques discussed in the first portion of this book in searching for and often successfully locating shipwreck remains. The task at hand now is to give you some basic groundwork material so that you may have a place to start in your search for shipwrecks.

Each of the chapters in Part III will represent a state (one chapter for each coastal New England state and New York) and in each I will give a detailed account of a few wrecks which are, to my knowledge, unlocated or salvaged. Hopefully each different type of vessel and situation will be covered herein and hopefully will stimulate some of you to dig into the history a little more and give wreck searching a try. If you choose to do so—good luck in your search!

9 Maine

THROUGHOUT the years the rugged and bleak coast of the state of Maine has claimed countless ships whose crews were unfortunate enough to be the victims of foul weather, raging seas, or sometimes of their own shipmates' fatal mistakes. Such was the case of the famed wreck of the "Circus Ship," the *Royal Tar,* in 1836.

The *Royal Tar* was a fine new steamer under the command of Captain Thomas Reed, one of the veteran captains of the New England coast. Her regular route was from St. John, New Brunswick to Portland, Maine and during the steamer's short career the Royal Tar made several trips back and forth between these ports. During the early days of October Captain Reed found himself forced to lay over at St. John more often than not due to some moderately severe weather and his patience with this foul weather was rapidly disappearing. On Friday, October 21st, with a slight clearing on the horizon, the *Royal Tar* pulled away from her berth and once again headed south. The cargo aboard the steamer on this trip was a strange one indeed. First there was the Burgess' World Famous Circus complete with wild animals, camels, horses, and "Mogul", an enormous elephant who was so large that he had to be stored on deck. The brass band of Dexter's Locomotive Museum was also aboard and as the vessel steamed out of the harbor at St. John the passengers and crew relaxed to the fine music of the band's musicians. There were seventy-two passengers and twenty-one crew members on board and together with the large cargo filled the vessel almost to capacity. After leaving the relative calm offered by the lee of the shore a strong westerly wind was encountered which intensified to such a degree that Captain Reed deemed it advisable to run into Eastport on Sunday the 23rd where the *Royal Tar* remained until Tuesday. When the steamer again put to sea, on the 25th, the weather had not improved considerably but time was money and the

Although the sidewheel steamer *Capitol City* was more than twice the size of the steamer *Royal Tar*, it is fairly representative of early steamboat design. The *Royal Tar* was lost off Vinalhaven Island in Penobscot Bay, Maine, October 25, 1836, due to a fire. *Photo courtesy of Peabody Museum, Salem.*

captain felt obliged to continue the voyage despite the unfavorable sky. Steaming across Penobscot Bay the captain felt better now that the ship was on its way again when suddenly, about 2:00 P.M., acting Engineer Marshall streaked into the pilothouse, his face as white as a sheet, and stammered to Captain Reed that the steamer must be stopped immediately as the boiler was out of water and was red hot. Captain Reed was dumbfounded. The Royal Tar had been two days in port and no one noticed that the boiler water was low? He immediately brought his vessel to a full stop and ordered her anchored when almost two miles from the Fox Islands. At this time the wind was blowing fairly strong from the northwest as Captain Reed and Engineer Marshall made their way to the boilers to begin the operation of taking on water. Before reaching there, however, the cry of "Fire" was heard by the men who rushed on to see what the cause and extent of the disaster was. Apparently, there were two causes to this fire: first, and of most importance, the water level in the boiler being extremely low caused the boiler to be red hot; and second, because of the added weight on the deck (of Mogul the elephant) wooden wedges had been placed below the deck to further support this weight and these wedges were in direct contact with the boiler. As the boiler became hotter the wedges began to char and then to burn, soon to be followed by the deck above. Regardless of the causes of the fire the results were disastrous. Panic reigned supreme among the passengers and even some of the crew. Captain Reed tried vainly to gain control to make an orderly escape from the burning vessel and he felt sick as he thought of the ship's boats that were left behind to provide enough room for the animals on deck. Of the two remaining boats, one was quickly grasped by about sixteen panic-stricken passengers, launched, and pulled away from the burning steamer. Meanwhile, those members of the crew that maintained their composure worked their way below to the fire engine but the smoke and flames quickly drove them back to the deck. The animals that were below deck died swiftly and quietly by choking on the dense smoke, almost a kind death compared to that awaiting the passengers above some of whom jumped overboard into the frigid waters of Penobscot Bay. The animals on deck, as well as the passengers, were in a frenzied state and all except Mogul, who could not be approached, were released to jump overboard. Suddenly the wind shifted to the southeast and the captain almost cheered for he now had the chance to slip the anchor and set the *Royal Tar*'s sails in hopes that the breeze would bring his vessel to the shore where the remaining passengers and crew could be saved. The mainsail and jib were quickly set but, unfortunately, as soon as the anchor was slipped the wind shifted back to the northward and the steamer began drifting offshore. To add to the ship's troubles the fire broke through the deck at about the same time and consumed both sails leaving the ship at the mercy of the sea. The fire on deck was too much for poor Mogul the elephant and in a fearful rage he broke his chains and leaped overboard and was last seen swimming for shore at full speed. Some of the more composed passengers still on board hastily threw together a makeshift raft of ladders and planks. They launced it with some difficulty and jumped over after it and those who were able to clamber aboard were to be seen no more. As the fire drove those remaining on board even closer to the point of jumping some enterprising men came up with the idea of hanging by a rope over the side. This would enable them to get away from the fire but would keep them out of the frigid waters which otherwise awaited them. Before long, several passengers were in this position and many found themselves in a bad way as others, whose ropes had burnt off, clung to whoever was handy to keep from falling in and drowning. Captain Waite, a passenger, supported a woman and a man for over an hour while clinging desperately to the rudder chain. Mr.

M. M. Fuller miraculously supported four persons for several hours while suspended from a rope off the stern which was wound around his leg and also his neck!

After being in this situation for a considerable time the revenue cutter from Castine arrived at the scene and through the efforts of Captain Reed and the crew of the cutter's boat a total of sixty-one passengers and crew were saved. Despite the seriousness of the conflagration which occurred and the panic which followed only thirty-two souls were lost.

An inquiry into this disaster held in the weeks after positively placed the blame on the Acting Engineer and attributed the loss of the *Royal Tar* to the gross neglect and carelessness of the second engineer Marshall who allowed the water in the boilers to become depleted causing the boiler to overheat excessively. The total property loss not including the vessel was estimated at $150,000. The elephant Mogul alone was valued at $7,000. His carcass some weeks later washed ashore at Brimstone Island.

The statistics of the steamer were as follows: She was built in St. John in April of 1836 only a short nine months before she met her fate at a cost of approximately $50,000. She was one hundred and sixty feet long and had a twenty-four foot beam and a registered weight of almost four hundred tons. Her owners were Mr. John Hammond (50%) and D. J. McLaughlin and MacKay Brothers & Co. (50%). Although her career was an extremely short one she was and still is remembered by local residents as having had one of the strangest cargoes ever seen by mariners in New England. Incidentally, when last seen the *Royal Tar* was in the vicinity of Saddle Back Light where she is believed to have sunk.

THE *CAMBRIDGE*

During the years following the 1850s the number of steam powered vessels on the east coast was significantly increasing. Although in later years there would be a clear distinction between freight carrying ships and passenger ships this was not the case with the early steamers which usually carried a little of both on every voyage. Such was the case of the steam side-wheeler Cambridge built in 1867 for the Bangor and Boston Line. She was not an extremely large vessel being only 1,200 tons burthen but was quite popular particularly in Bangor and Bucksport the ports to which she brought many essentials to the few local residents. The vessel was valued at $100,000 and, as seems to be the case with many of the early coastal steamers, was insured for only about half of her value or $50,000.

On her fateful journey to oblivion the Cambridge was carrying

This is an unusual stern view of a sidewheel steamer on blocks. Pictured is the sidewheeler *Cambridge* of 1867 whose career spanned almost two decades. On a northbound voyage to Bangor and Bucksport in 1886 the steamer met with disaster on a small ledge known as the Old Man off Port Clyde, Maine. *Photo courtesy of Peabody Museum, Salem.*

assorted hardware valued at about $100,000 and a few passengers. The vessel was bound north for Bucksport and Bangor under the able command of Captain Otis Ingraham, a veteran skipper of the line. As the vessel steamed north on February 10, 1886, she was under the charge of Captain William T. Rogers, first pilot of the Cambridge, another veteran of this line who had been sailing in these waters for over twenty years. Although it was nighttime and very dark and chilly as only a February night can be, Captain Rogers was confident in the course that he had followed for many years. He chatted with the helmsman about the trip and about his family but neither man was much for idle chatter and soon silence returned to the men in the pilothouse as the vessel continued steaming along the desolate shoreline. The silence was suddenly broken by a deafening crash. Captain Rogers was dumfounded. There were no obstructions or rocks on his regular course and, according to the helmsman, that was the course that was being run at the time of the accident. The pilot immediately checked his watch and noted that it was 4:45 a.m.—he was right on time according to his usual schedule to be off Port Clyde, Maine. In fact, he was off Port Clyde but he was about a mile closer to the shore than he should have been and had struck the ledge locally known as "The Old Man." The vessel immediately heeled to starboard and began to fill. In the cabins the passengers and crew were thrown from their berths to the deck but were able to maintain their composure and most quickly dressed and worked their way forward to the saloon. In the meantime, Captain Rogers was hastily rechecking his figures to find out why his vessel should have been so far off course but he could find no apparent reason for it. The saloon was quickly filled with anxious people all of whom wanted to know where they were, what had happened, and most important what was going to happen to them. Captain Ingraham kept the group cool and explained to them the procedure of lowering the boats which, he stated, would be the means of their escape as soon as it would become light. As dawn approached the rescuing operation was begun. The women were placed in the first boat to leave the steamer which landed them at Burnt Island. In short order, all of the passengers and crew were transferred from the *Cambridge* and landed at that island and later were taken from there to Rockland from whence they were sent on their way to their original destinations.

The vessel began going to pieces within days and the scene around the ledge was one of many boats eagerly searching every cove and inlet along the rugged coast in the quest for anything salvagable from the cargo or the vessel. While this salvage was going on the crew of the *Cambridge* had gathered and were all trying to determine the exact cause of the disaster. It was decided that since a large portion of the cargo consisted of nails and iron sled shoes this bulk of iron objects might have affected the compass and caused the vessel to be steered off course while those in the pilothouse thought she was still following her regular course. This may or may not have been the case and there was some disagreement on exactly where that portion of the cargo was stowed but, regardless of the cause, the result was already settled and the vessel was to prove almost a total loss where she settled on the Old Man Ledge off Port Clyde. During the weeks that followed there was a larger amount of salvage carried out on the cargo and it was thought that all together almost forty percent of the goods would be recovered—leaving more than half of the cargo plus the vessel on the bottom awaiting the ambitious diver who will discover the steamer's bones.

THE *WASHINGTON B. THOMAS*

Toward the end of the 19th century, as the days of the sailing vessel were becoming numbered, a last ditch effort to bring back the sailing vessel as more economical than a steam powered vessel saw the growth of these wind powered ships into huge behemoths capable of carrying tremendous amounts of cargo in bulk form from one port to another. One of the larger vessels of this period was the five-masted schooner *Washington B. Thomas*. The *Thomas* was built in Thomaston, Maine in 1903 and her dimensions were formidable indeed. From the head of her bowsprit to the transom at her stern she measured two hundred and eighty-six feet long; her beam measured about forty-nine feet. She was two thousand, six hundred and thirty-eight registered gross tons and had a depth of hold of twenty-two feet giving her a carrying capacity of over four thousand tons. Her history was a short one, indeed, culminating in her loss near Stratton's Island, Maine on June 12, 1903, the same year that she was launched!

Her second and last trip began at Newport News, Virginia on June 3rd. She was bound for Portland, Maine with a cargo of four thousand, two hundred and twenty-six tons of coal to heat the homes of hundreds of Maine residents during the coming winter. Her master, Captain Lermond, was not without experience in sailing vessels and his new command pleased him greatly. As the *Thomas* set sail from the Virginia port there were fifteen persons on board including Mrs. Lermond. The sails quickly filled and the five-master left at a good rate for the New England coast. After being at sea only a short time the captain found his

The five-masted schooner *Washington B. Thomas* is one of a very elite group of vessels who have had the misfortune to sail for fewer days than were necessary to build them. Only sixty days after her launch the *Thomas* stranded and became a total loss on rocks near Stratton's Island, off Cape Elizabeth, Maine. *Photo courtesy of Peabody Museum, Salem.*

ship fogbound and this weather continued throughout the duration of that fateful voyage. On June 11th the fog broke briefly and the men aboard the ship were able dimly to make out the ragged Maine coastline and one spot they knew well, Richmond's Island, south of Portland. Captain Lermond was in a quandary as to what to do next. He could not safely navigate along the treacherous shoreline of Cape Elizabeth in this dense fog but he was not at all pleased about the possibility of putting to sea in this weather either. He finally decided that it would be best to tack away from the shore for the time being and these orders were quickly carried out to bring the *Thomas* a few hours run from the coast. About 7:00 P.M. on the 11th the captain decided to return to the shore and see if the fog had lifted for good. Finding this not to be the case he decided to anchor near the shore and wait out the weather before proceeding to his destination. The captain sailed along the coast taking soundings and finally brought his ship to anchor in very deep water. The fog was exceedingly thick at the time and the captain had only a very vague idea of where his ship was but he felt it best not to continue sailing around these dangerous waters taking the chance of collision with another vessel or, even worse, running on one of the many sunken ledges in the vicinity.

The *Thomas* remained at this anchorage throughout the night and all of the next day, spotting the shore only once in all this time. When they did spot shore the crewmen recognized the lighthouse on Wood Island which was to the northeast of the ship's location. They knew that they were fairly close to the shore again but Captain Lermond was sure that the anchorage was an adequate one for his vessel and decided to remain there. By nine o'clock on that day (the 12th) a breeze came up from the southwest and with an unkind rapidity soon worked itself up to a full gale. The crew and the captain were becoming quite concerned now and justly so as the Thomas soon began to drag her anchor across the bottom heading straight for the lighthouse that they had previously seen. As the huge vessel continued to drag the captain saw clearly the impending doom that awaited them if they hesitated any longer. He gave the order to set the main and started forward with his crewmen just as the sea began to break over his entire vessel. No matter how hard they tried even the bravest and strongest men of his crew were unable to get forward and slip the anchor chain. For nearly an hour they continued to drag shoreward while the crew desperately tried to move forward. Finally, about ten o'clock the *Thomas* was carried onto the outlying ledges off Stratton's Island, near Biddeford, and began thumping on the bottom with great force. Almost immediately, the enormous vessel began to break apart.

The crew scrambled wildly into the rigging while Captain Lermond headed to his cabin to rescue his wife. A huge sea rolled over the *Thomas,* nearly washing the captain overboard, and as he regained his feet he saw that reaching his cabin might be impossible. Several more combers engulfed the vessel in rapid succession, finally driving the captain to the rigging in an act of desperation in his wild fight for life. He wanted desperately to try again but the crewmen convinced him that there was no hope for his wife as the cabins below deck were by now completely flooded. As he clung to the rigging the captain wept both for the loss of his beloved wife and the loss of his fine ship and several times during the wild fury of the gale he was tempted to give it all up as it seemed there would be no further meaning to his life if he survived. He had only few moments of rest, however, as his men turned to him in search of an encouraging word as he was the most experienced aboard and his saying that they would be saved would mean everything to each man aboard.

The night was a long one, indeed, with none of the crew getting any sleep at all as the incessant pounding of the sea threatened to break apart the *Thomas* at every moment. As dawn broke, miraculously, every member of the crew was still in the rigging and still alive but the incessant pounding of the waves continued to rock the vessel back and forth filling these men with a fear that could only be imagined by a seaman in peril of his life at sea.

Help was on its way, however, as in the early light of the dawn local residents spotted the ship's perilous position and rushed to town to call out for volunteers to man a surfboat to make an attempt to save the imperiled men. So severe was the force of the sea and wind that it was a task of hours for the boat to be launched and even more hours to span the short distance to the ledge upon which the Thomas was impaled. The efforts of the boat crew were rewarded and the life savers were able to remove nine crew members safely before they deemed it necessary to run back for the shore and safety. The trip back to shore was equally full of danger and the sea promised at every minute to dash the little boat and its occupants to pieces. But, as good fortune would have it, the surfboat and its occupants were landed safely toward the end of the afternoon and the nine survivors were quickly rushed to local homes to be fed and cared for as Maine residents know well how to do, having succored many victims of shipwrecks over the years along their perilous coast.

As for Captain Lermond and the remainder of the crew still on board the *Thomas*—they were forced to spend a second harrowing night aboard the dying schooner. Gale force winds continued to blow throughout the second night and many of the crewmen were in very bad shape after hanging to the rigging for longer than thirty hours. On the morning of the 14th of June, the residents again rushed to the shore to see if the remaining men were still in the rigging of the doomed ship. They counted the figures in the foremast shrouds and were pleased to see that there were five remaining persons, as there had been when they last visited the ship. With great haste they set about their final rescue attempt. The seas had moderated considerably and the volunteer crew had little difficulty in launching the boat and in reaching the ship. Removing the final group of survivors was not as easy a task as it had been on the previous day and the men were found to be generally injured and suffering from exposure. The mission of mercy was accomplished, however, despite the severity of the weather and all of the remaining survivors were safely transported to shore and safety.

The local residents eyed the wreck with a common thought. There was an enormous quantity of coal lying out there for the taking and free coal was always better than paying for it. Unfortunately, the best laid plans of men often go awry and such was the case with the hopes of the residents to salvage the coal aboard the schooner. Within a few days of the original stranding the *Thomas* began showing the final signs of its demise. The hull was continually smashed by the incessant action of the waves and in short order the once proud five-masted schooner was reduced to splinters and a pile of coal. One can imagine the sight of the masts, one by one, falling by the board with a thunderous crash and the mass of wreckage of all descriptions wash ashore at many points along the coast. As the hull and the hold of the *Thomas* filled with water and the sea continued its unending battering the inevitable result was that the hull should fall outward with a roar and allow the coal to be scattered at the whim of the waves and currents present in the area. Thus ended the very short history of one of the larger schooners ever built in New England. From the day of its launch to the day of its demise it served as a fine example of bulk-carrying sailing vessels—for just sixty days of history.

The water surrounding the ledges off Stratton's Island averages about forty to sixty feet in depth and in some spots even ninety feet of water can be found. For those interested in searching for the remains of the *Thomas* there are a few facts to keep in mind: the wind direction (which will push the remains in the direction it is blowing), the cargo (as there was over four thousand tons of coal aboard it would seem logical that near the center of wreckage there is a very large pile of coal), and local water conditions (currents, extremes of tide, etc.). In view of the size of the vessel and the area involved, it would seem likely that this wreck would be a fine one, indeed, to search for.

This ends a brief description of some exciting wrecks which have taken place along the Maine coastline. Because of the barren and rugged nature of this coastline the loss of lives from shipwrecks which have occurred in these waters has been high and the number of wrecks here has also been quite high. Diving in this state will require extra protection in terms of a thicker-than-average wet suit but other than this the normal range of equipment will be adequate.

10 New Hampshire

THE *CELESTE*

A S we travel down the New England coastline the next state we come
to is New Hampshire. This state has the distinction of having the
least amount of shoreline of any coastal state in the United States. What
there is of it, however, is almost as rugged as the neighboring Maine
seashore. Marine disasters in New Hampshire are fewer than in the other
New England states because of the limited number of ports here but the
severity of these disasters is equal to disasters in any state.

In the 19th century it was common for much coastal trade to be carried
on by foreign shipping interests who often followed a pattern known as
triangular trading. This simply consisted of taking goods from port A to
port B and then, instead of returning directly to port A, the vessel would
pick up another cargo for port C at which point a final cargo would be
taken aboard for the trip home to port A. Very often the foreign vessels
engaged in our coastal trade were of British registry and such was the case
of the schooner *Celeste*.

On January 5, 1866, the *Celeste* set sail from St. John, New Brunswick
with a cargo of fine Canadian lumber for Boston. She was under the able
command of Captain Rainard who, unknowingly, was never to set foot
on land again but that was always the chance one took when living the
rigorous and dangerous life of a seaman. This schooner was a relatively
small vessel, only about one hundred and ninety tons, and was sailed by a
crew of three in addition to the captain. Captain Rainard was familiar
with the northeastern coastline of New England having traveled this
route many times before with a similar cargo. Moreover, he was familiar
with the problems often encountered in traveling during the winter
months along these shores. Any mistake by him or by a member of the
crew could be more than dangerous—it would most likely be fatal as the
water temperature would allow a man to survive only a few minutes if he

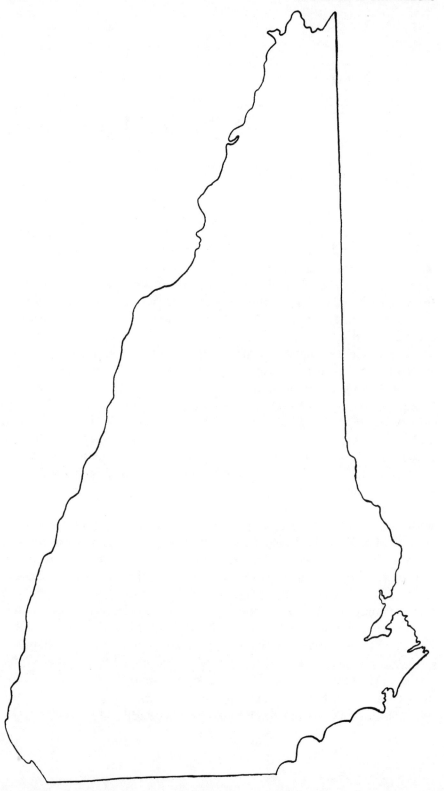

was so unlucky as to be washed overboard or if the vessel foundered at sea. The weather during the trip had been generally about average with a constant, frigid wind almost following the *Celeste* since her departure. The seas had been moderate to heavy until the 20th or 22nd and with an unusual fury they had picked up considerably as his schooner approached its destination.

On Thursday, January 25th, the weather had its way and the little vessel was at its mercy. Wave after wave crashed over the ship and in short order knocked her down on her beam ends throwing the captain overboard as it did so and causing the rudder to become unshipped. The captain was lost and the remaining men were in a perilous situation but the battering waves finally washed away the deck load and slowly the vessel began to right itself, full of water, and the men were enabled to

Shipwrecks similar to this unidentified brig have occurred along the entire length of the New England coast for well over three centuries. A disastrous fate such as the one pictured here caused the loss of the small schooner *Celeste* off the mouth of the Hampton River, New Hampshire, on January 26, 1866. *Photo courtesy of Peabody Museum, Salem.*

clamber into the rigging. The little *Celeste* was at the mercy of the elements now and drifted about for hours as the frozen crew remained in the rigging clinging to anything that they could grasp and each praying that he would not be the next to be washed overboard. The men remained in this shaky condition throughout the night unaware of what disaster was yet to befall their little ship. Toward daylight some even began praying for the end to come quickly and bring relief from their pitiful suffering.

The end for the *Celeste* was, indeed, very near at hand. On Friday the little schooner struck a group of submerged rocks near the mouth of the Hampton River. The sea began making a complete breach over her and it seemed to the men that all was lost. As harrowing as the night before had been it seemed now to have been mere child's play compared to the suffering they were now forced to endure. But they endured and, as they could see the shore from their perch in the rigging, they knew that it would only be a matter of time before they would be noticed and a rescue attempt made to save them. What they didn't know was that they had been observed for some time before striking the rocks and the onlookers from shore didn't dare attempt to put out a boat in such a raging sea. One among them, Captain D. F. Nudd, could stand watching them no longer after only a short time at the scene and through his courage and determination he was able to organize a volunteer crew to man a surfboat and at least make an attempt to save the unfortunate men. It was a considerably risky task to launch a boat here but nevertheless it was done successfully and the brave rescuers were soon pulling at the oars toward the ill-fated ship. With a smooth dexterity the surfboat approached the *Celeste* and neatly plucked all the crewmen from the rigging and began the trip back to shore.

Within a few short hours the *Celeste* showed signs that the end was near and soon there were only fragments on the beach to remind the local residents of the heroic deed that had been performed that day by one of their own. Captain Rainard, who was the owner as well as the master of the *Celeste*, was the only casualty of the entire disaster but even one life is too much to give when it means leaving a wife and many children without a husband and father.

Interested persons might well seek out these sunken rocks at the mouth of the Hampton River, near the town of Hampton, New Hampshire. There are apt to be more than one set of ship's bones resting here and the opportunity for a good artifact, even from a small vessel, is ever present and awaits the diver with imagination and ambition.

THE *IVA BELLE*

In the annals of great storms in the New England area the researcher will very quickly find the date of November 27–28, 1898 to appear many times in reference to vessels lost. This was the date of the famous *"Portland* Gale" which was named after the largest vessel to be lost during that storm. But the *Portland* was by no means the only vessel lost in that hurricane. Disaster struck the coastline from Rhode Island to the most northerly section of Maine and a total of nearly two hundred ships were lost, destroyed, sunk, dismasted or otherwise damaged by the ferocity of this storm. Everywhere along the coast life savers were kept busy rushing from one vessel to another in an effort to save lives and preserve property. This was also the case in New Hampshire and one vessel in particular, the schooner *Iva Belle,* is illustrative of the efforts made by men everywhere during that storm to save their fellow men.

When the storm first struck the *Iva Belle* she was in the vicinity of Portsmouth, New Hampshire bound south from Belfast, Maine. She had been at sea several days and, being a relatively small vessel—only a two-masted schooner—when the storm broke she took a severe beating which brought fear to the hearts of the strongest men in her crew. The *Bell*'s captain was familiar with the features of this section of coastline and knew exactly where he was at the time. He decided that the safest thing to do was to run for Portsmouth Harbor for a safe refuge from what he thought was just an overly strong northeaster. Little did he know that at other spots along the New England coast the wind was blowing or would soon blow in excess of one hundred miles per hour.

As the *Iva Belle* proceeded toward its safe refuge the crew made a fatal mistake while entering the outer harbor and in short order the vessel struck bottom near Odiorne's Point early on the morning of the 27th. The seas immediately began to attack the little schooner with a fury never before felt by this captain or crew. With immediate threats of extinction facing them the captain and crew lost no time in scampering up the foremast rigging. How long they were there before a patrol from the Jerry's Point Life Saving Station spotted them was never accurately determined. While the rigging with each successive wave threatening to pull them from their grasp each minute must have seemed like an hour to the imperiled crewmen. The members of the shore patrol battled their way back to their station through the fierce winds and reported the situation of the vessel to their commander who quickly issued orders to gather the beach apparatus and proceed to the vicinity of the disaster to

The bulk of American coastal trade in the mid to late years of the nineteenth century was carried by small schooners such as the *Alice Wentworth* (pictured). Like a thousand others, including the *Iva Belle*, these vessels were subject to the mercy of the wind and waves. During the infamous "Portland Gale" of late November 1898, the *Iva Belle* met her fate on the rocky shores of Portsmouth, New Hampshire. *Photo courtesy of Peabody Museum, Salem.*

save the stranded men if any chance of this was at all possible. Word of the disaster quickly spread throughout the town and some persons felt that the ship as well as the men might be saved if immediate action was taken. Many of the local residents went to the life saving station to offer assistance in carrying equipment to the beach while others volunteered to man the tug *Piscataqua* under the command of Captain Perkins to make a run to the schooner to aid in the rescue of the men and the vessel. The life savers arrived at the scene before the tug, complete with their Lyle gun, lines, breeches buoy apparatus and shot line. The Lyle gun was quickly set up and the first shot attempted but the wind caught the line and carried it away from the vessel to land ineffectually in the surf.

Meanwhile, the *Piscataqua* left her dock in the early afternoon and those on board soon found that the gale was increasing to the point where their vessel could be in peril as well if they were not very careful. A second shot fired from the beach was equally as ineffective as the first and as the life savers pulled the shot line back to the beach they were fearful that all their efforts might be for naught. This would be the case if they didn't reach the men aboard the schooner soon. The *Iva Belle* was showing signs that it would soon go to pieces as the captain and crew clung for dear life to the shrouds. The sheer agony that these men were forced to suffer is indescribable but they did not give up hope as they could see that the life savers were valiantly fighting to save their lives as strongly as they themselves were. The tug was within sight of the *Bell* now but Captain Perkins could see that it would be next to if not impossible to save the vessel if, indeed, even the men could be saved. He decided to stand by the wreck and if the life savers could not soon get a line across the vessel he would, if he had to, launch a boat from the tug in an effort to save life. As the life savers set up the Lyle gun for their third shot the gale momentarily abated somewhat and with a resounding cheer from the life saving crew the men aboard the Belle watched the shot line land right in the middle of the rigging, only an arm's length away. The shot line was quickly attached to the heavy line for the breeches buoy and the crewmen of the *Bell* began the difficult and tricky task of pulling the line out to their ship. There was still the danger that the heavy line and shot line might become parted due to the strain upon them from the incessant waves but fate smiled upon these men and in short order the heavy line was grabbed by the anxious sailors of the schooner and attached to the mast. One by one the three crewmen and the captain took their turn at the breeches buoy and, to the pleasure of all on shore, they were safely landed on the beach.

The shipwrecked men were all taken to the life saving station where they were fed and clothed as they related their tale of the anxious moments suffered by all as they hung in the rigging and awaited whatever their fate would be. All, needless to say, were more than merely thankful to be alive and ashore as the gale continued to increase in its ferocity every minute. The *Piscataqua* remained in the vicinity of the *Iva Belle* until Captain Perkins saw all the men saved, and for awhile longer in hope that the gale might pass and offer him the chance of a good salvage if the vessel could be pulled off the rocks. The volunteer crew aboard the tug soon convinced him that the vessel would prove a total loss and he reluctantly complied with their wishes to leave the scene and head back for the wharf. For awhile fears were entertained for the tug as it was growing dark and Captain Perkins should have been back earlier but at 9:00 P.M. the tug pulled into her berth in Portsmouth Harbor and many local residents were much relieved to see him and his volunteer crew alive and well.

It was the opinion of Captain Perkins and his crew that the *Iva Belle* would go to pieces before morning and this, in fact, proved to be the case. This left the survivors of the disaster with nothing more than the clothes they had on so the life savers took it upon themselves to secure passage to Belfast for the men. There was nothing to salvage from the *Iva Bell* and the wreck, being small, was quickly forgotten (even though the storm was not).

Today the rocks around Odiorne's Point hold the bones of several shipwrecks including the *Iva Belle* and an ambitious diver would do well to look into this area as a possible source of artifacts from these wrecks. It's at least worth a good look!

11 Massachusetts

WITH the second longest coastline of the coastal states in New England, Massachusetts has a considerable number of treacherous spots upon which many a fine ship ended her days. With Boston a central port for ships of all sizes and a hub of trading activity from the earliest days of our union, one can imagine the considerable amount of shipping traffic passing along the coast at any given time. Cape Ann, to the north, and Cape Cod, to the south, stood as silent sentrys seemingly guarding Boston from these ships and it is no wonder that both of these capes are littered with the remains of many gallant vessels. Prior to the construction of the Cape Cod Canal vessels bound south to New York were forced to make an important decision after passing the outer cape. They could sail out to seaward making a large semicircle around the great Nantucket Shoals (which extend outward from the island of Nantucket to a distance of about twenty miles eastward and forty miles southward) or chance running the gauntlet of Nantucket and Vineyard Sounds bordered on the shore side by the lower cape and the Elizabeth Islands and on the ocean side by Nantucket and Martha's Vineyard islands. This area has seen countless shipwrecks over the years and is one of the most dangerous areas in New England.

THE *CITY OF COLUMBUS*

Possibly the worst disaster ever to occur in this area was the destruction of the steamer *City of Columbus* which struck on a sunken ledge known as the "Devil's Bridge" off Gay Head, Martha's Vineyard on January 18, 1884. The steamer, bound for Savannah, left Boston at 3:30 on the afternoon of January 17th. She was under the command of Captain S. E. Wright, a veteran of the Boston and Savannah Line, who had been with the line since 1869 and had successfully made one hundred and ninety-

one voyages without a single mishap. He was proud of that record and well he might be for he spent much of his time plying the waters of Nantucket Sound and Vineyard Sound in going and coming between Savannah and Boston. On this evening he would make perhaps the only mistake of his entire career—a costly one indeed!

The *City of Columbus* was a fine and staunch vessel built in Chester, Pennsylvania by John Roach & Son in 1878 for the Ocean Steamboat Company of New Jersey. The Boston and Savannah Line aquired her in September of 1882 to run in conjunction with the steamer *Gate City* also of that line. When built the steamer was rated A1 for 100 years and her iron hull had withstood six years of constant use with no ill effects. She was a large ship measuring two hundred and seventy feet in length, thirty-nine feet of beam and drew seventeen feet of water at her deepest point. Her registered tonnage was one thousand nine hundred and ninety-seven tons and she was valued at $300,000, a large sum indeed for that period, and her owners only carried $250,000 insurance on the vessel. She had accomodations for eighty-four first class and forty-five second class passengers plus the crew. On the ill-fated voyage she had fifty-nine first class and twenty-two steerage passengers aboard plus her regular crew of forty-five officers and men.

As the steamer quietly crossed Cape Cod Bay, Captain Wright had no reason to believe that this passage would be anything but routine and in a normal fashion she passed the Pollock Rip Lightship at 10:00 P.M. and the Cross Rip Lightship at midnight. It was noted at this time that the wind was blowing west-southwest and strong but the night was clear and there was nothing to hamper the helmsman's visibility. The night was cold and after passing Nobska Light and when off Tarpaulin Cove Captain Wright decided to go to his cabin to get warm. This was at about 3:00 A.M. the captain having been on the bridge throughout the journey, except at dinner, since the steamer left Boston about twelve hours earlier. Captain

The steamer *City of Columbus* was the victim of the worst single marine disaster ever to take place off the shores of Martha's Vineyard Island in Massachusetts. On January 18, 1884, with a full complement of crew and passengers, the unfortunate steamer ran off course and struck the treacherous ledge known as the Devil's Bridge off Gay Head with a loss of nearly one hundred lives. *Photo courtesy of Peabody Museum, Salem.*

Wright left the pilothouse in charge of the Second Mate, Augustus
Harding, went into his cabin (which adjoined the pilothouse) and sat on
the floor, leaning against the radiator to keep warm, and with his head
inside the pilothouse. For some reason unknown to us, the Second Mate
left the pilothouse next, leaving the pilot, McDonald, alone in the room.
The cold was penetrating and before long the pilot was thoroughly chilled
so he decided to set the wheel with tiller ropes so that he could go over to
the smokestack and warm his hands. Unbelievably, he spent fifteen to
twenty minutes away from the wheel.

As the ship surged ahead untended there was a flood tide running down
the sound and the wind, blowing a gale by this time, was acting on the
starboard bow. Perhaps it was these factors that caused the vessel to veer
from her routine course but in any event the *City of Columbus* did just
that. It is unclear by the accounts of the disaster just when the Second
Mate returned to the pilothouse and the pilot returned to the wheel but
suddenly and without warning Captain Wright heard the Second Mate
yell, "Port the helm!" to the helmsman and, thinking that his vessel was
approaching another and in danger of collision, he ran into the pilothouse
and quickly gave the command to shift "Hard aport." As he entered the
pilothouse, the trained eye of the captain spotted the Devil's Bridge buoy
to port, about two points forward of the beam and about three hundred
yards distant. Within seconds the *City of Columbus* struck
something—what it was eluded the men at the time—which later proved
to be the "Devil's Back," the outer extremity of the Devil's Bridge. As the
vessel struck, with comparative ease, the captain glanced at the
chronometer and noted that it was about 3:30 A.M. The pilot was of the
opinion that the vessel struck two or three times before she stopped.
Whether it had struck only once or multiple times the end result was the
same—the vessel was resting on the ledge in a dangerous position. Gay
Head Light shone through the windows of the pilothouse bearing south
half east as the wind howled and the fury of the storm increased.

The shock of the vessel striking the ledge had dealt a death blow by
breaking up one of the iron plates in the forward hold. A general alarm
was immediately rung and throughout the ship there was a hum of
activity. Captain Wright immediately ordered the engines reversed and
the steamer backed, by his account, about two lengths and then stopped.
The engineer on duty gave a somewhat different account of the events.
He reported feeling the vessel strike, getting bells to reverse, which was
done, and then getting bells to go ahead, which drove the vessel back
upon the rocks. Exactly which report was correct will never be known

but the engineer was reported to be the only person who disagreed with the captain's story.

Captain Wright immediately ordered the jib hoisted and endeavored to head the *City of Columbus* to the north but his vessel bellied forward and listed over to port. All together it was probably only about twenty minutes after striking that the steamer listed. After he sounded the alarm and had ordered the engines reversed, the captain proceeded to work his way aft to tell the passengers to keep cool and to order the boats made ready for lowering. As he was doing so the vessel listed, settled aft, and later righted. The vessel had only remained listing for about ten or fifteen minutes but during this brief period the passengers that were already awake began to panic. At this time, having been briefed by the captain as to the perilous situation facing them, the crew ran through the ship in an attempt to awaken any passengers still sleeping.

The crewmen attempted to launch port boat #6 which was immediately capsized in the high seas that were by now making a complete breach over the vessel. Five more boats were released and all but one were broken up immediately by the angry waves. The one boat that might have made its way free of the steamer quickly came to its own bad end—none of the boats were plugged and this one filled and sank with no hesitation.

When the Columbus first struck, the after hatch was washed clear of the ship allowing water to enter the inner parts of the vessel and this was what caused the vessel to settle by the stern. Fearing the worst, the Mate, Second Mate, Chief Engineer, and Fourth Engineer headed for the life raft which was secured to the top of one of the houses on deck. The raft was reached and made ready to launch by Edward Fuller (First Mate), Augustus Harding (Second Mate), Archibald Morrisson (Chief Engineer), Wm. Murray (Third Assistant Engineer), Wm. Fitzpatrick (pantryman) and Richard Sullivan (deckhand). A heavy sea struck the steamer just as the men were about to launch the raft and washed it and its occupants overboard. The raft went in one direction and the former occupants in the other. No one was able to effect a rescue, however, as the situation was every man for himself and by now there were about forty persons atop the houses and in the rigging.

The mountainous waves continually battered the steamer in the early morning hours driving more men to the tops of the houses and then to the rigging. Scores of persons were washed overboard as they came on deck but nothing could be done to save them as the entire ship's complement were in danger of being washed over at any second. About 7:00 A.M. the steamer's deck began to break up with a thunderous roar. Those still alive in the rigging cringed and clung a little tighter to their perilous perches fearing that at any moment the ship might break apart and they would be mercilessly thrown into the frigid water to die a horrible death. The last house on deck served as a platform for Captain Wright, the Farnsworth boys, seaman White and steward Pitman. At about eleven o'clock this house was destroyed by the waves but its terrified occupants all scrambled safely into the rigging.

A discouraging statistic concerning the persons still on board the steamer when dawn arrived was that all the women and children except the two Farnsworth boys were lost. The effects of exposure on those persons in the rigging were soon becoming apparent and several persons, one by one, fell from their perch to the tumultuous water below. The survivors of the night began to gain hope of rescue as a steamer was sighted at about seven or eight o'clock in the morning, on the other side of the sound but their hopes were dashed as the steamer continued on its journey, bound east, without even slowing down. This steamer later proved to be the *Glaucus* under the command of Captain Maynard Bearse whose excuse was that he didn't see anyone in the rigging of the wrecked vessel and he was in a hurry to get to port. The action of this captain speaks for itself and those who survived the disaster were extremely critical of him and his crew.

At about 10:00 A.M. a boat from the Gay Head shore approached the wreck and took off seven persons (one of whom died later). In order to be saved each person in the rigging had to jump into the icy water and swim to the boat to be hauled aboard. Only the most hardy could survive this ordeal but few left in the rigging succumbed after surviving the night. A second boat left Gay Head between noon and 1:00 P.M. and the revenue steamer *Dexter* arrived at the scene at about 12:30. The sea was still running high when the *Dexter* arrived and she was forced to anchor about two or three hundred yards away. The cutter immediately lowered a boat under the command of Lieutenant Rhodes and on their first run to the wreck they managed to remove seven persons. The first of the Gay Head boats brought a total of twelve persons to the *Dexter,* one of whom died after being transferred to the cutter.

The second boat from Gay Head was unable to rescue any persons but their actions in coming out in an attempt to save lives was commended by all. Lieutenant Kennedy, of the *Dexter,* took the ship's gig and returned with four or five persons while Lieutenant Rhodes' crew rested to make a second trip. Captain Wright was the last living person taken from the ship to survive. Lieutenant Rhodes returned to the steamer in an effort to remove the two remaining persons from the rigging who were in such bad shape that they could not jump into the water to be rescued.

With a determined look on his face, Lieutenant Rhodes decided to swim to the ship and personally remove the men from their perilous position as long as any hope remained for their lives. On his first attempt the young lieutenant was struck by a floating timber and had to be hauled back to the *Dexter's* boat. He was returned to the cutter but after resting for several hours decided that he would try again and, because of his determination, the Captain of the *Dexter* allowed him to do so. On this second attempt Lieutenant Rhodes was successful but, unfortunately, the men in the rigging both died, one just after being placed in the cutter's boat and the other after they had reached the safety of the *Dexter*. All together there were twenty persons alive and one dead put aboard the *Dexter*. All but three of the twenty who were alive when brought aboard survived. It must have been a woeful sight, indeed, to see the *Dexter* steam into New Bedford with such a sad tale to tell.

The ledge where the *City of Columbus struck*, the Devil's Bridge, is actually a double ledge. These hidden rocks extend northward from the Gay Head Light and the outer portion, or Devil's Back, is about an eighth of a mile from shore with deep water on each side. The outer ledge runs west about a half mile and then north for a few hundred yards. The buoy marking the ledge is placed about a quarter of a mile west of the western extremity of the ledge. As the vessel sat at this desolate location it became evident to those watching that she could not stand the strain of the tremendous seas still pounding her and by 6:00 P.M. it was felt that she would quickly go to pieces. There was but one small section of the bow visible above the water plus the masts and rigging but the remaining portions of the steamer were entirely under water. The exact position of the City of Columbus was north one-half west from Gay Head about a mile and a half from shore. More important, the steamer lay almost a quarter of a mile inside the buoy marking the ledge and not outside as it should have been if the buoy were seen to port when the vessel struck and sunk.

In all, twenty-three persons were saved and ninety-seven were lost. The life raft, which had been washed overboard, came ashore at Cedar Tree Point, ten miles from Gay Head, on Sunday afternoon, with no sign of life aboard. The one lifeboat not destroyed landed miraculously at Gay Head about 7:00 P.M. with five persons aboard: two passengers, two crewmen, and Quartermaster McDonald.

During the following weeks some interesting information was discovered about the disaster itself and the condition of the wrecked steamer. It was determined that the buoy marking the Devil's Bridge was considerably off its normal station. In fact, it was found to be at least a quarter of a mile inside of its normal anchorage but, even so, that did not provide an excuse for the disaster as that would place the ship even further off her correct course. On January 23rd, the first attempt was made to survey the wreck using divers but the current was running too swiftly to permit the divers to remain on the vessel. On the following day diving operations were resumed at two o'clock. The divers, Duncan and Ollsen, reported the following: 1) all the upper works of the vessel, above the deck, were gone; 2) not a single stateroom remained on deck; 3) there were scattered heavy timbers covering the entire length of the deck and this prevented access to the lower levels of the ship; and 4) no bodies were seen by either diver. By 2:30 that afternoon the wind picked up to another gale which meant the cessation of diving operations for this day.

Wrecker Scott was contacted about doing a critical survey of the *City of Columbus* to see if the vessel could be saved and after making a dive his diver had the following facts to report. First, a hole was found forward measuring about three feet square and approximately twenty feet from the stem, and around this hole were several smaller ones forward and abaft of it. Second, there was a perpendicular crack found near the foremast which appeared fairly extensive. All about the port quarter by the main rigging there were portions of the smokestack and machinery covering the deck. Apparently, aft of the boilers near the bottom of the hull there was no material damage but there were numerous cracks. When the diver moved to the other side of the ship he found an extensive crack under the foremast which might meet the one previously found on the starboard side and, if this were the case, it would mean that the vessel was broken in two at that point. Further forward on the port side there was extensive damage probably resulting from the fact that when the vessel listed it was to port.

In the summary report, the diver was pessimistic and his opinion was that the vessel's hull was generally too much damaged to make it worth raising. On February 3rd, diver Duncan made another dive on the site of the wrecked steamer and made an amazing find and recovery—the ship's safe. He found the safe on the starboard side of the vessel abaft the mainmast. It had moved almost seventy-five feet from its proper location and was free of the wreckage making the job of raising it an easy one. Those aboard the lighter anxiously surrounded the safe as it was about to be opened since rumors had already begun (as they usually do following any shipwreck) to the effect that there was a considerable amount of money aboard but, alas, when opened the safe was found to be virtually empty. Throughout the week following this find the diver continued to ramble through the wreckage in hopes that some sort of salvage could net the divers some monetary gain. Finally, on February 12th, all further efforts to recover property from the steamer were abandoned due to the extreme conditions in the vicinity. On the second of March, just forty-four days after the *City of Columbus* struck on the Devil's Bridge, the hull of the vessel mysteriously disappeared, perhaps devoured by the sands around the ledge. It was an untimely and unfitting end for such a gallant vessel but one that was not reserved for steamers alone, as we shall see, in these dangerous waters of the Massachusetts coast.

THE *JASON*

The sandy shores of Cape Cod bear no resemblance whatever to the rugged and rocky coast of Maine but each, in its own way, can be equally devastating. Sandy shores have claimed an unbelievable number of men and ships through the years and many stand out as being particularly spectacular disasters. The British ship *Jason* lost on Cape Cod's Peaked Hill Bars in 1893 is a fine example.

For the many years before she was lost, the *Jason* could be found in all the international trade circles. She was a fine ship of iron construction which was originally built in Scotland in 1870. She was owned by two brothers, A. & J. H. Carmichael, of Greenock, Scotland and was believed to be one of the finest ships of her type in existence at the time of her demise. She was registered as one thousand five hundred and twelve tons burthen and carried various cargoes to varied ports throughout her long life. At the time of her loss she was under the command of Captain McMillan who had not been with her at the start of the voyage but who would ultimately be the man to blame (as the captain of a ship usually is) for her wreck. The firm of Charles Hunt & Company of Boston had consigned for the vessel which was carrying a cargo of ten thousand eight hundred and sixteen bales of jute to the Ludlow Manufacturing Company of Boston. As this cargo was of considerable value it was insured (at offices in New York) but unfortunately for the owners there was apparently no insurance on the *Jason* itself.

The story of the loss of the *Jason* actually began on February 17, 1893 at which time she set sail from Calcutta, India for Boston. While crossing the Indian Ocean toward the Cape of Good Hope, at the southern tip of Africa, the *Jason* was caught in a typhoon of monumental fury and, although surviving that disaster, she was dismasted totally and was forced to put in at Mauritius, a small volcanic island east of Madagascar. The ship remained at that port until September while being refitted for the rest of the journey. Almost one thousand bales of jute were required for payment but that could not be helped and in early September the *Jason* once again set out for Boston. Her voyage from Mauritius to the coast of the United States was uneventful which pleased her new captain no end.

As the ship approached the Massachusetts coast the weather grew foul again and the morning of the 5th of December found the ship beating into an east wind and into the teeth of a sleet and snow storm. Visibility was patchy for awhile and the captain could see the shore of the cape but try as he might he couldn't beat around the tip of Race Point faced with this seething gale. Why he did not choose to lay offshore until the weather moderated is not known but after three months at sea on a voyage which had now consumed ten months in its entirety the men were probably more than ready for a change. It was a change they got, too, as they spotted the cresting breakers just before striking on the outer bar of the Peaked Hill Bars. It was about 7:15 P.M. and darkness had already fallen like a shroud concealing the vessel's position from all but the most penetrating eyes on shore.

Earlier in the day the surfmen from all the stations on the outer arm of the cape had been discussing the weather and, in his heart, each feared another night spent in what were often unsuccessful attempts to save men from the sea. At about 7:25 the surfman on patrol from the Pamet River Station burst through the door of the little refuge hut used by three men and announced his discovery of a large ship just offshore in the breakers. With a rapidity that was the result of experience the crew gathered together their beach apparatus and boat and began their half mile trek through the snow down the beach to the spot opposite where the *Jason* was stranded. About this time the fury of the storm was causing unbelievable damage aboard the *Jason*. Her main and mizzen masts were carried away almost as soon as she struck bottom. The crewmen, probably not being knowledgable about such disasters, had taken to the rigging of the mizzenmast thinking that to be the safest place to go in times such as this. By 8:00 P.M., only a short time after the ship struck, bales of jute began to wash ashore indicating that the ship might already be breaking up.

The surfmen finally reached that spot on the beach after an arduous trip through wind blown snow drifts and the biting, freezing sleet which had begun again. To attempt to launch the boat in this weather and sea would have been insanity, reasoned the captain of the station, so with little other

Although the remains of the British ship *Jason* did not come ashore from the famous Peaked Hill Bars off the outer fringes of Cape Cod, they would have resembled the remains pictured here of an unidentified wreck at Novaressisk if they had. Little can compare to the awesome end that claimed all but one member of the *Jason*'s crew when she broke in two in a December storm of 1893. *Photo courtesy of Peabody Museum, Salem.*

choice at the moment, the men set up a camp on the beach, to wait for the weather to moderate enough for them to launch their boat or use the Lyle gun. Sometime around 10:30 P.M. the *Jason* began to break apart with a thunderous crash heard by the surfmen even over the violence of the gale. The men jumped to their feet and peered into the gloom looking for any sign of life at all but there was nothing. The ship was now suffering the final throes which could only lead to her going to pieces under the devastating effect of the mountainous waves crashing over her. Wreckage had been washing up on the beach for hours and suddenly among the remains a body was spotted. Half the crew dashed along the beach to see if they could find any others while the remainder immediately came to the scene of the discovery. It was found to be a boy, miraculously alive, and after beating on him to restore his circulation and giving him some spirits his saviors heard the tale of the agony of his mates and himself while in the rigging.

Being trapped in the rigging of a vessel in distress is bad enough by itself but when the calamity befalls the ship in the frigid winter months the agonizing pain of hanging in the ship's upper works is multiplied one hundred times over. The survivor identified himself as Samuel J. Evans, nineteen, of Greenock. He told the surfmen that about twenty men had been thrown over at once and he inquired as to how many others were saved. When he learned that he alone had been found he cried in despair over losing his shipmates. Without a word, some of the surfmen bundled him up and took him to the station for further comfort.

About midnight, two interesting events occurred: 1) The men from the Highland and Cahoon's Hollow stations arrived at the scene (having been notified earlier by the captain of the Pamet River Station that a large ship was ashore at this place) and 2) The two sections of the vessel apparently broke away from each other and the waves sent ton after ton of cargo and other wreckage ashore. Quickly, the life savers scattered to search through every bit of wreckage for another survivor but after searching the shore for several miles in each direction and finding no one, these men returned to the camp to see if they could be of more assistance there.

As if satisfied that it had destroyed the *Jason*, the gale now began to diminish and the crew of the life saving station quickly went to work in setting up the Lyle gun and other beach apparatus. They could not know whether or not there were any living persons left on the remains of the ship. Their first shot went wide of its target and the line was retrieved with some difficulty due to the floating wreckage in the water. Another shot, again unsuccessful, showed that the gale was not yet ready to give the life savers any chance at all. But persistence pays, they say, and on the third attempt the line fired straight and true and fell across the remaining bits of the *Jason*. The men waited to feel a tug on the line which would indicate the possibility of life still aboard the doomed ship but they waited in vain as no sign of any survivors was forthcoming.

As dawn approached the men could dimly make out what appeared to be the *Jason*, lying offshore about two hundred yards distant. They could make out the form of a man in the foremast rigging but he did not move or make any sign that might indicate that he was still alive. As the sun rose higher in the sky the surfmen could see what the full effect of the winter gale had accomplished. The *Jason* lay, heeling over to starboard, in two sections with nearly one hundred yards between them, a complete wreck. With no further possibility of aiding men or ship the surfmen gathered their equipment and began the arduous trek back to their station through the snow.

Once again the sea had won and this always left the surfmen more than just sad because they knew that with an unkind regularity this type of shipwreck would occur again and again on these desolate shores. When they questioned the sole survivor further they learned that there had been twenty-six persons aboard the *Jason*. An attempt was made later that day to remove the frozen body still in the *Jason's* rigging but the high seas prevented the vessel from being approached until the following day. In all, there were only twelve bodies recovered before the wind shifted to an offshore breeze which would carry cargo and wreckage away from the shore of the cape and would bring some of it to land on the Nantucket shore in weeks to come.

The desolate shore of the area around the Peaked Hill Bars has claimed an unbelievable number of ships, at least fifty of which I have knowledge of, and probably hundreds of unrecorded marine disasters have taken place here to be forgotten by all but the descendants of early Cape Cod families, particularly those who had ancestors who were involved with the life savers and the life saving stations. The shifting nature of these sand bars makes searching the area an ambitious undertaking, indeed, but with the use of electronics and modern searching methods surely the bones of many of these lost vessels, if not the *Jason* itself, will be uncovered for the anxious student of marine history.

THE *MERTIE B. CROWLEY*

As the twilight of the era of sailing ships approached, those who still believed in sail over steam rose to new heights in terms of the dimensions and carrying capacity of schooners. For all practical purposes, the six-masted schooner was the largest successful schooner ever built. There was one seven-master built, the *Thomas W. Lawson*, but it proved to be a "white elephant" and was never copied by another company anywhere. There were eleven six-masted schooners built, mostly in the state of Maine, and of these eleven none survived the rigors of the sea (every one was burned, wrecked, or lost when within twenty years of age).

The *Mertie B. Crowley* was not the biggest of these giant ships, by far, but she was impressive, indeed, measuring two hundred and ninety-six feet in length by forty-eight feet in width (beam) and having a draft of almost twenty-four feet. Like most of her sister ships she was built in Maine, at Rockland, in 1907 for the Coastwise Transportation Company. She was of wooden construction and had a registered tonnage of two thousand eight hundred and twenty-four tons. Equipped with all the modern conveniences of the day, the *Mertie B.*, as she was often called, even had her own steam power for handling the sails. This allowed her to be manned by a crew of only thirteen men. No cost was spared in her

The *Mertie B. Crowley*, or *Mertie B.* as she was commonly known, belonged to the very small group of sailing vessels to ever carry more than five masts. Since competition between steamers and sailing vessels was beginning to bring about the end of the latter, it was felt that the only way for sailing vessels to compete was by making them larger. This idea never proved successful but left the ambitious wreck searcher with several fine shipwrecks to discover and explore. *Photo courtesy of Peabody Museum, Salem.*

construction and such a fine job was done that when she was launched she was valued at over $160,000. In fact, she was so valuable that many experienced captains desired to have command of her but that privilege fell to Captain William Haskell. She was designed to carry many types of bulk cargo but predominantly carried coal from southern ports to her home port of Boston.

The fatal voyage of the *Mertie B.* began at Norfolk, Virginia when she set sail for Boston with a considerable load of coal on board. This trip was to be a treat for the members of the crew since Mrs. Haskell was aboard and that meant a good trip for all as she was quite fond of the crew that had served her husband well on many voyages. This was, indeed, more than a routine trip for hardly had the ship left port when she was found to be fog bound, a dangerous condition in the winter in the days of considerable coastwise traffic. The thought of a collision became an omnipresent thought in the minds of all aboard and put more than a slight damper on what was to be a happy trip. The captain deemed it prudent to heave to when off the ocean side of Long Island, New York and for several days the schooner was without sight of land knowing not exactly where she was. A break in the dense fog permitted the captain to see what he thought was Shinnecock Light near Montauk Point and he set his course to the north hoping to spot the light on Block Island when the fog lifted again. This proved to be his first mistake. The light he had spotted was, in fact, the light on Block Island but this he would not learn until it would be too late to do anything about it.

It was and still is an eerie feeling sailing through the fog not knowing exactly where you are going and, even though a lookout was always on duty, you could never tell when a steamer or even another sailing vessel might come crashing through the dense fog and cause a collision that might mean the end to your ship, his ship, or even both. It has happened time and time again from the days of the earliest sailors to the modern day disaster of the *Andrea Doria* and *Stockholm* in which the larger *Doria* was lost due to just such a collision. When sailing in fog everyone on board would be exceedingly quiet, each straining his ears for the sound of an approaching vessel or for the fog signal indicating a lighthouse ahead, and the aura of impending doom was all about the *Mertie B.* that night of January 22, 1910. During the late watch the captain was called on deck as another light had been spotted and his expert knowledge of the coastal lights was needed so that no error would be made by a lesser-in-command. The captain immediately came on deck and scrutinized the dim light which, he surmised, was that of Block Island's southeast light. This was his second mistake. The light was from the tower at Edgartown, Martha's Vineyard, whose south shore the *Mertie B.* was now approaching. The captain decided that he should stay on deck as his vessel would be approaching the devilish waters and shoals surrounding the southern approaches to Cape Cod before long and these waters would require his undivided attention until the cape was passed. As dawn approached the *Mertie B. Crowley* suddenly, and without warning, even from the lookout who could see no further than the head of the bowsprit, struck firmly on the shoal known as the Wasque Shoal, south of Martha's Vineyard Island. It was then about 5:30 A.M. on Sunday and the ship was in a bad position, indeed, being on the westerly end of the shoal and almost three miles distance from the nearest shore. This location was about one mile inside the buoy which marks the southern extremity of this shoal and the captain knew, although he still did not know exactly where they were, that his ship was in for a very bad time.

Almost immediately, the gigantic combers native to this shoal began tearing his ship to pieces, ferociously sweeping the deck of the schooner, tearing away the ship's boats and almost everything else that was loose on deck. The deck became icy and treacherous as the flying spew of each wave quickly froze in the sub-zero temperature that a January night in Massachusetts is noted for. In moments the gallant captain knew that it was a lost cause and his ship would surely be demolished. Without hesitation, he ordered his men to take to the rigging. He would follow as soon as possible but he still had his wife to think of and he set out with determination to reach the cabin and rescue her. He found this to be more easily thought than done.

He tried to time his run to the cabin between the oncoming waves but he was thrown to the deck several times and very nearly pulled over into the raging sea that surrounded his ship. At the same time the cargo hatches were ripped from their hinges and the weight of water from enormous seas began to fill the spaces below the deck. Captain Haskell finally managed to reach the cabin and extricated his terror-stricken wife but the next task, getting her into the rigging, would be a near impossible feat for any man to accomplish. Many times Mrs. Haskell gave up all hope and pleaded with her husband to leave her and save himself but he adamantly refused and continued in his determined efforts to save both of their lives. The schooner was actually riding a little better now that the water had filled the lower portions of her and the two Haskells did, indeed, manage to make their way to the forerigging. Once there, the captain noted that all his men had scrambled to safety and for this he was grateful but the future promised nothing for these men whose chances of rescue were slim, if any.

As dawn became daylight the men aboard the *Mertie B.* were given hope by the fact that the fog quickly burnt off and they could see, and hopefully be seen from the shore. Captain Haskell quickly recognized the island and realized exactly what his mistake had been but that was of little concern now. Everyone now in the rigging was lashed to either the mast itself or a crosstree and for good reason as many of the waves crashing on the schooner reached to the height of their perilous position. They had chosen well to seek the safety of the forerigging as, at about ten o'clock, the *Mertie B.* broke in two and anyone aft of the mizzenmast would surely have been lost in the boiling sea below. As the schooner broke in two, the three after masts were carried away and her stern section settled almost immediately.

The great combers continued to pelt the *Mertie B.* with an endless savagery but one of the crewmen spotted a boat coming out and the men knew that all was not lost until they let it be lost. There were actually several fishing boats that set out from Vineyard Haven on that memorable morning in an attempt to rescue survivors, if there were any to be saved, from such a fine vessel. Only the most knowledgable and fearless men would venture out in such a sea but there were many such men at the Vineyard who knew what it meant to be stranded at sea. Of all the vessels which came out, there was only one which could and would dare crossing the shoal area in such a rescue attempt—the thirty-two foot sloop *Priscilla*

The effect of the relentless pounding sea on the hull of a stranded ship will quickly destroy even the most staunch of vessels. Pictured is the whaling bark *Wanderer*, which had the bad luck of stranding on rocks off Cuttyhunk Island in Buzzard's Bay in 1924. Although she appears to be taking it all in stride, she was eventually destroyed by the same waves that carried her to distant and exotic ports of call. *Photo courtesy of Peabody Museum, Salem.*

under the command of the ever-courageous Captain Levi Jackson—and after making the decision to run the gauntlet and make every effort to save the men aboard the stranded schooner the captain and crew did just that!

The *Priscilla* was brought up as close as possible to the *Mertie B.* and four boats launched to see to it that the men were removed from the rigging. Those on the schooner would have to jump, in turn, from their perilous perches to the boats below and in a brave fashion the first to jump was Mrs. Haskell who did the job quite well and then fainted in the boat. One by one the men jumped and only one missed his boat and had to be hauled from the water. Finally, only one man, Captain Haskell, remained aboard the dying schooner. When his turn came he too jumped and successfully landed in one of the *Priscilla's* boats. All were brought back to the fishing vessel and graciously thanked Captain Jackson for his efforts but he would accept no thanks until they were all back on the island. The trip back took several hours and was almost as harrowing as spending the night in the *Mertie B.*'s rigging but, finally, all were landed at Edgartown safe and sound and very much glad to be alive.

Wrecker Scott was called in and he made an attempt to salvage anything salvageable from this once proud vessel but the *Mertie B. Crowley* was doomed; the strong winds and seas prevalent here soon finished her, leaving only fond memories for the captain and crew. The area in which the *Mertie B.*'s bones lie is still a mean one, indeed, and like all large and sandy areas in which shoal water predominates, the contours of the bottom change almost daily. This is no reason to give up hope, however, and the shifting sands of cape waters have more than once turned up fine relics of the past and will continue to do so in the future. It's probably well worth a look!

Just as a note of interest, three other six-masted schooners of the original eleven built and lost are located within thirty miles of the remains of the *Mertie B.*, including the largest ever built, the *Wyoming*. If that doesn't serve as testimony to the treacherousness of the waters of Massachusetts and, particularly, in the area of Cape Cod, I don't know what does. My suggestion is let's get with it and find some of these fine shipwrecks!

12 Rhode Island

RHODE Island, the "Ocean State," although the smallest of all of the United States of America, has been an important hub of maritime activity from the earliest days of our country's history. With Narragansett Bay one of the best natural harbors on the eastern seaboard it was obvious that shipping interests would find this an important refuge from the often too prevalent nor'easters. Although the coastline cannot begin to compare with the ruggedness of Maine's shoreline or the treacherousness of Massachusetts' sandy cape, numerous reefs abound and have brought many a ship's crew to their knees, or worse.

THE *BENJAMIN BUTLER*

At the western extremity of the Ocean State stands a small community known as Watch Hill. Between this town and Fisher's Island, New York, a mere three miles distant, lie some of the most dangerous waters in the entire state. Strong currents, hidden rocks, and deep water offer a potential for disaster seldom equalled anywhere. This spot affects the adjoining sounds, Block Island Sound to the east and Long Island Sound to the west, by creating strange and powerful currents which have often caused problems for the large number of ships plying the coast from New York to points north and vice versa. Competition between the nightboats, or floating palaces as they would later be called, and even among the cargo-carrying steamers was mentioned before and it was often due to this competitive attitude of captains that many vessels ended their days on the bottom of the sound. Such is the case of the cargo schooner *Benjamin Butler,* of Providence, Rhode Island, lost in collision with the steamer *Thetis* on February 25, 1870. As New Englanders know well, there is nothing to compare with the fury of a New England winter gale with its icy chill and furious gusts.

149

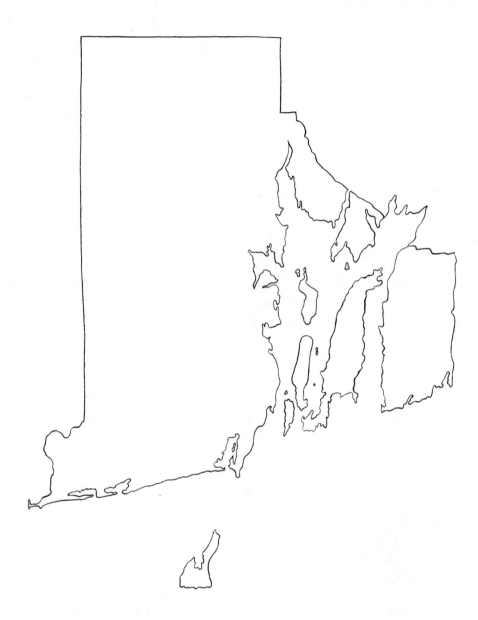

The *Thetis*, of the Neptune Line, of Providence, was one of the better freight carriers available due in part to her master, Captain Gale, whose reputation for safety plus speed was enviable, indeed. On that fateful Friday night when the steamer blew her shrill whistle announcing her departure and cast off her lines for the trip south a gale force wind was already building. The trip down Narragansett Bay was uneventful but the captain couldn't help but notice a dense fog bank that rapidly engulfed all of the surrounding shoreline as his steamer rounded Point Judith. True to form captain Gale reduced his ship's speed and began to sound his whistle warning all ahead that he was coming.

About this time the schooner *Benjamin Butler,* also of Providence and Wickford, was cautiously proceeding up the sound her hold filled to capacity with a cargo of coal loaded at Elizabethport, New Jersey bound north to heat the homes of numerous Providence residents. The *Butler* was a carbon copy of countless coasting schooners of this day having been built at Middleton, Connecticut in 1856, of one hundred and twenty-five tons registered burthen and rated A2 by Lloyds. She was under the command of Captain Theodore Fowler, of Wickford, and was handled by a crew of four men. The captain of the *Butler* was not fond of sailing in this type of weather but, as was and still is often true, the profit motive overcame the captain's better judgment. Passing Watch Hill, Captain Fowler found himself engulfed in the same dense fog as Captain Gale though neither knew of the other's presence. At about 1:30 A.M. as the strange hand of fate brought the *Butler* and the *Thetis* closer together for their fateful meeting the vessels were still invisible to one another. According to the log of the *Thetis*, the steamer's helmsman spotted the schooner about 1:45 A.M. as she suddenly appeared out of nowhere directly in the path of the *Thetis'* bow. It was no contest, indeed, as the size and momentum of the *Thetis* as compared with the *Butler* was easily overpowering. With a deafening crash, a splintering of wood and the screams of men knowing that their doom has been sealed, the ships met for the first and last time. This meeting would be brief, loud, and final for the men aboard both vessels.

The helmsman aboard the *Thetis* was numbed more by the shock of the crash than by the cold. He had done what he could in the few brief seconds before the impact—threw the wheel amidships, stopped and reversed the engine—but the steamer's inertia was more than enough to cause her bow to cut through the schooner like a hot knife through butter. Aboard the *Butler* confusion reigned. Every man knew what had happened and also the probable consequences. The thought of being lost at sea in the month of February when exposure would claim their souls in

The schooner *Benjamin Butler*, like many other small schooners, ended her days on the bottom of the ocean. Perhaps, in a manner similar to the wreck of the schooner *Alva*, pictured here, her masts and standing rigging stood to mark her location. *Photo courtesy of Peabody Museum, Salem.*

less time than imaginable was a horrifying thought, indeed. Captain Gale, of the steamer, immediately called for his vessel to be stopped and made ready to lower a boat to search for any survivors of the calamity. The schooner had been struck just aft of her main rigging and sank like a rock.

The search party remained in the area until almost 2:30 A.M. but succeeded in rescuing only the mate of the *Butler*. Sadly, but responsibly, the steamer's captain called off the search with the knowledge and understanding that any further search would be futile—there would be no more survivors! When all the facts were gathered and weighed a day or two later it was determined that the location of the disaster was approximately five miles east of Watch Hill and that neither vessel or captain were at fault. The ship's lanterns aboard the *Butler*, although burning, were presumed to be so badly iced up that it would have been impossible to see her and avoid the disaster. Also, as the steamer was travelling at a reduced speed due to the weather conditions there was no recklessness involved on the part of Captain Gale. For the families of the lost men and captain there was little consolation, however, as neither vessel nor cargo which were lost were insured leaving nothing but memories of loved ones to hold.

This is but one of many disasters that have occurred in Block Island Sound and the problem of weather and sea conditions in this area is one which may plague mariners forever.

THE *ACHILLES*

Block Island, a desolate and isolated little island off the Rhode Island coast, lies at the eastern extremity of Block Island Sound. At her northernmost end a sand shoal presents a danger to vessels passing too close. From her southwestern to southeastern corners the shoreline is like no other found in New England. Cliffs as much as three hundred feet high overlook this rocky southern shore and countless ships have discovered, to their dismay, that to run aground here is almost certain doom for vessels and men alike. The passage between Block Island and Point Judith (the nearest point of mainland) is deep and very navigable, being almost seven miles in width, but a remarkable number of vessels have mistaken the light on the northern tip, Sandy Point, of Block Island for the light at the southern tip of the mainland at Point Judith. The result is inevitable—Point Judith can only be passed safely to the south and Sandy Point Light can only be passed safely to the north. Point Judith and Sandy Point both have numerous shipwrecks along the shore! Our interest here, however, is the southern shore of Block Island and a wreck of considerable interest to the wreck searcher.

The steamer *Achilles* was an early example of two innovations in marine construction. Although built in 1870 in Chester, Pennsylvania, she was of iron construction rather than the more popular wooden construction. Also, she was powered by a screw propeller rather than side wheels or paddles. The age of modern shipbuilding had arrived. Her dimensions were impressive for her day: almost one hundred and ninety-seven feet in length, thirty-nine feet of beam, and she drew thirteen feet of water. She was almost seven hundred and sixty-four registered gross tons and when first built carried a Lloyd's rating of A1 for ten years. Powered by a one hundred and fifty horsepower engine and

On June 6, 1887, the iron steamer *Achilles* came to grief on the desolate south side of Block Island, R.I. Like the steamer *Algiers*, pictured here, she was of the new breed of ships that would see the end of wooden hulls and paddle wheels. *Photo courtesy of Peabody Museum, Salem.*

having a cargo capacity of one thousand tons made her a very popular and ever busy vessel, indeed. As with many vessels of her day she was primarily employed as a coal carrier from points south to the cold New England towns who reciprocated by shipping machinery and manufactured goods south. On her final voyage she was bound from Philadelphia for Newburyport, Massachusetts with a cargo of coal which was probably destined to be used by her owners, the Philadelphia and Reading Railroad Company. The *Achilles* was under the able command of Captain Stokley Warrington who was anything but a newcomer to the trecherous waters of New England.

On the night of June 6, 1887 Captain Warrington was at his post in the pilothouse of his steamer peering into the gloom ahead which was the result of the usual prevailing fog bank found throughout Block Island and Long Island Sounds. He proceeded ahead with caution despite his knowledge of these waters as he was only too aware of the ease with which Block Island could be suddenly encountered if he allowed his alertness to wane for even a few moments. His course was set to pass by the outside of the island and then set a course for Buzzard's Bay and thus pass into Vineyard Sound by daybreak. At the bow, a member of the crew was posted on watch to scan ahead and "sing out" if any danger was spotted so that it might be avoided. So dense was the fog, however, that it was only seconds after the lookout called out the alarm, "Breakers Ahead!" that the captain heard the awesome sound of his ship's hull grating on a rocky bottom and then, with a start, her forward motion stopped. Captain Warrington had a funny feeling that he had, indeed, found Block Island, but not in the manner that he had hoped.

The clam and coolness of an experienced crew was evident as the engine room flooded and the great iron ship began to settle to the bottom. As it turned out, the Achilles was very near Lewis Point, Block Island, on the island's southern shore. The captain checked his watch—it was 9:30 P.M. His first problem was to see to the safety of his crew, then his ship, and finally, himself. As luck would have it, the somewhat perilous position of the ship was spotted from shore and shortly after the stranding Captain Warrington and his entire crew were standing on the cliff overlooking his damaged ship below.

The next morning, at first light, an accurate estimate of the damage to the ship would be made and it was observed at that time that the *Achilles* was resting in about ten feet of water on a rocky bottom and in an extremely bad position if a storm should come up. As soon as was possible, word was sent to the *Achilles'* owners and to the Merritt Wrecking Company of New York with whose assistance the vessel might be saved. The islanders wasted no time in living up to their reputation of never letting a good wreck lie and they began the task of separating the *Achilles* from her coal cargo. A few days passed before the wreckers, complete with divers, arrived at the scene and already about half of the cargo had been removed. The first step for the wreckers was to make a complete survey of the vessel both topside and underneath and the results of this report would determine the outcome of any salvage attempt. Divers descended with some hope as the condition of the hull from above appeared good. Luck was not with the *Achilles,* however, and from the woeful looks of the returning divers Captain Warrington knew that there would be little hope of saving his ship.

The ship had shifted from its original position and now lay broadside to the beach in about twelve feet of water. The divers reported large holes in the vessel's bottom and, even worse, a broken keel. There was little more that the wrecking crew could do and since they worked on a "no cure, no pay" basis their departure from the island was as rapid as their arrival. It was on June 12th, only a short six days after the stranding, that the *Achilles* was officially abandoned as unsalvageable. The next large storm did its very best to insure that the iron-hulled Achilles was firmly in Neptune's grasp and little more survived to be "scoffed up" by eager islanders. Her remains today would be a fine find, indeed!

The area of Lewis Point, Block Island is not inaccessible to the ambitious diver. What will be required is a boat since carrying gear over the rough terrain is an almost impossible task. Visibility in the area is generally good and the depth is fairly shallow which has good and bad points in its favor, easy to dive and search but probably only small parts of this gallant ship remain. However, keeping in mind what is possible on shallow water wrecks such as the *Lydia Skolfield,* this wreck would definitely make a fine dive and must necessarily yield many treasures to the ambitious wreck searcher.

THE *LARCHMONT* & THE *HARRY KNOWLTON*

Generally speaking, when two ships collide at sea the outcome is usually that the smaller vessel (if severely enough damaged) sinks while the larger vessel limps into the nearest port to be hauled out on the local marine railway, refitted and sent back into service. From time to time, however, the smaller vessel overcomes the size difference and fatally strikes the larger vessel. Such is the case in point: the collision between the steam side-wheeler *Larchmont* and the coal schooner *Harry Knowlton.*

The scene of the disaster was, once again, Block Island Sound on another freezing and blustery February night in 1907. The *Larchmont,* of the Joy Line, left its berth at Providence about 7:00 P.M. on Monday, February 11th. She was, by all reports, one of the finest side-wheel steamers of her day, being well over two hundred and fifty feet in length and having thirty-seven feet of beam. She was of wooden construction and weighed in excess of one thousand six hundred tons. She boasted three deck levels and two masts in addition to her large vertical beam engine capable of one thousand horsepower and normally travelled at a speed of up to twelve knots. A routine passage carried her between Providence and New York city and local inhabitants all along the route knew well her twin stacks and distinctive form. Her safety was entrusted to her master, Captain George W. McVey, an able man for the job. On her final trip to destiny she carried approximately $45,000 worth of general merchandise and a large number of passengers.

When the *Larchmont* left the safety of her berth there was a fairly strong northwesterly breeze coming up and the passengers quickly retired for the evening on what they thought would be a rough but routine trip. It was almost 11:00 P.M. when the huge steamer rounded Point Judith and headed into the teeth of what was now almost a full gale.

At this time, unknown to anyone aboard the *Larchmont,* a small coal schooner, the *Harry Knowlton,* was plowing through the rough seas on her passage up the sound. Her master, Captain Haley, had decided to run for the shelter of Narragansett Bay for a safe anchorage and he was running with the wind under all the canvas his little ship would take. The *Knowlton* was a small schooner of three hundred and seventeen tons and only one hundred and twenty-eight feet in length but a full cargo of coal aboard must have given her a considerable amount of momentum in her own right.

On Monday, February 11, 1907, the sidewheel steamer *Larchmont* left her berth at Providence bound south for New York city. When about three miles from Watch Hill, R.I., she was struck and nearly cut in two by the coal schooner *Harry Knowlton.* The death toll from this disastrous collision was nearly one hundred eighty lives. *Photo courtesy of Peabody Museum, Salem.*

The two-masted schooner *Annie F. Kimball,* pictured here, is nearly identical to the schooner *Harry Knowlton,* which struck and sunk the steamer *Larchmont.* It is hard to believe that such a small sailing vessel could cause the sinking of a steamer that was twice her size. *Photo courtesy of Peabody Museum, Salem.*

After the *Larchmont* had safely passed Point Judith Light Captain McVey had retired to his stateroom leaving the responsibility for the ship's safety to the hands of his best helmsman. When the steamer reached a point about three or four miles from Watch Hill the Pilot made note that there were two sets of lights off their bow. One, he knew, was the lighthouse at Watch Hill Point and the other, he surmised, was another vessel proceeding up the sound. He continued to observe these lights for several minutes and decided that they were from a schooner but it appeared that the schooner was having some difficulty as it was yawing back and forth. The alert helmsman adjusted the course of the *Larchmont* to assure her safety but he noted in disbelief that the schooner remained on her collision course despite his course changes.

One can only imagine the conversation between the steamer's

helmsman and pilot as they watched the schooner approach closer and closer to what they felt would be her impending doom. With a terrific crash and the sound of glass breaking everywhere, the schooner struck the steamer on the port side just forward of the paddle box and with such an impact that the little schooner did not stop until it had travelled more than half way through the *Larchmont's* breadth. Then, as suddenly and swiftly as she had struck, the *Knowlton* was gone and where she had been there was a huge gaping hole through which thousands of gallons of water were rapidly pouring.

Without hesitation, the pilot signalled the emergency with several short blasts of the steam whistle. Captain McVey was in the pilothouse in no time at all seeking to know the cause of the emergency. He was aghast when he saw the damage his fine ship had received and as the steamer began to settle to starboard he didn't hesitate for a second before giving the order to lower boats. He knew his valiant vessel would quickly fill and make its trip to the bottom and the fear that gripped his mind must have been awesome. As the ship settled further to starboard the lifeboats on that side were practically launching themselves and those on the port side were getting further away from a possible launch attitude with every passing second. With assistance from the pilot and helmsman, Captain McVey commandeered one of the starboard boats in an attempt to come around to the port side (which was now the high side of the doomed ship) and rescue any passengers stranded there. Their task was an impossible one, however, as the gale prevented them from being able to round the bow into the wind. Unknown to the captain, some panic-stricken passengers had managed to launch four of the boats on the port side which proceeded to drift away at the mercy of the wind with only three or four passengers in each. Within thirty minutes it was all over and the *Larchmont* began her final plunge to the bottom.

But what of the fate of those aboard the schooner? When the *Knowlton* struck the steamer an equal pandemonium erupted among the schooner's crew. After all, they had struck a large sound steamer and everyone knew that the sound steamers were almost impossible to sink. Their schooner, they knew, was sinking and if they didn't do something quickly they would soon earn themselves a watery grave. Quickly the men began to work the pumps in earnest and they were even holding their own until off the small village of Quonochontaug at which time they were forced to leave their little ship in the boats.

The survivors from the steamer spent a harrowing night, indeed. They were not seamen and in the prevailing gale were completely at the mercy of the sea. Many who had deemed themselves lucky at surviving the sinking died of exposure during that terrifying night on the sound. Just before 6:00 A.M. on the following morning, a boy, the first survivor of the disaster, struggled to reach the light keeper's house at Sandy Point, Block Island. The alarm was quickly spread throughout the island and the islanders, who were no strangers to searching for survivors of shipwrecks and whose compassion in such cases was nearly unequalled, quickly gathered for a search. They had little hope, however, as all it would take would be a shift in the wind to keep any boats or wreckage from reaching their shore. All together, there were only nineteen survivors of the disaster. This raised a question as to a practice which had been common for many years and was about to cease, namely, the practice of carrying the only copy of the ship's passenger list on board the vessel. It was estimated that almost one hundred and eighty persons (including the crew) were aboard the *Larchmont* that fateful night which meant that more than one hundred and sixty lives were lost. To determine who was at fault in such a calamity as this was almost a waste of time; the damage had been done, the lives had been lost, and now $250,000 worth of steam side-wheeler lay on the bottom of Block Island Sound for all time.

To complete this account there are several facts which will be of interest to the wreck searchers. First, the approximate location of the disaster: according to reports the incident occurred about three miles from Watch Hill Point at about 41°16'00" North latitude, 71°49'18" West longitude. I have heard that the wreck has been located in fairly deep water in this vicinity but any ambitious wreck searcher would search out all such rumors and confirm or deny them for himself. Second, if you seek further background information on the vessel itself, such as a layout of the decks, etc., you will find that the original name of the steamer was the *Cumberland* and she was built for the International Steamship Company. Good searching!

13 Connecticut

T HE state of Connecticut, squeezed tightly between the state of Rhode Island on the east, and New York on the west, played an equally important role with her neighbors in the early days of maritime trade. Although not an industrial or trade center for shipping, the wealth of small but safe natural harbors that Connecticut possesses saved many an imperiled vessel by providing safe refuge from the frequent and violent nor'easters already mentioned. The ports of Stonington, New Haven, New London, Norwich and several others were seemingly situated in just the right place at just the right time on many occasions. As steamboats increased in size and numbers, many of these harbors became regular overnight stops for the voyagers, a fact which helped to increase the popularity of that mode of travel. After all, who could turn down an exciting sea cruise with the chance to see new places for a seat on a dusty train or coach ride.

THE *CITY OF NORWICH*

Several steamship lines had their beginnings in Connecticut and many adopted names such as the Norwich and New York Transportation Company. One steamer of that line, the *City of Norwich,* should be of interest to wreck searchers and is one of the subjects of this chapter. Built in 1862 and being fourteen hundred tons burthen you might suspect that she was one of the larger vessels of her day. Actually, she was only medium sized as the technology of the 1860's was beginning to turn out some really large craft. The *Norwich* was what you would have to call an average steamer of the line and carried out her routine passage from Norwich to New York with enviable regularity—that is, until April 18, 1866. There was an ominous haze on the horizon as the *Norwich* left her berth early that morning. The trip to New York only took about six

161

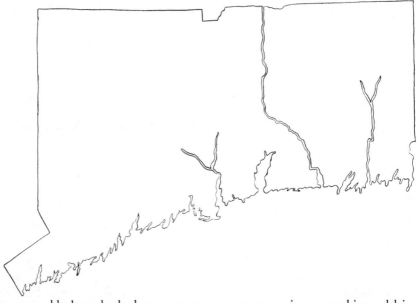

hours and below decks her passengers were more interested in grabbing a few hours rest in their staterooms than in walking about on the deck in the early morning haze. The pilot, Mr. Tracy, who was in the pilothouse at the time noticed that the slight breeze that had accompanied the ship from Norwich was beginning to show signs of becoming a good little blow. The weather report called for moderate weather, however, and he decided that he was probably making something out of nothing. Shortly before 4:00 A.M. the pilot spotted a vessel's lights dimly about three hundred yards ahead. He immediately brought the *City of Norwich* to port, slowed, stopped and then reversed the engines but to no avail. Within seconds, the bow of the schooner *Gen. S. Van Vlient* smashed into the port side of the *City of Norwich.* Tracy immediately roped the wheel and dashed out of the pilothouse to survey the damage to his vessel.

The steamer had been struck just forward of her port gangway and so great was the impact that the guards on the port wheel of the steamer were torn away. As he watched, the schooner slowly turned as the breeze caught her sails and the schooner's bow, which had been wedged in the steamer's side, popped out and revealed a gaping hole in the *Norwich*'s hull through which all of Long Island Sound began to pour. The pilot wasted no time as he knew the full extent of the damage and exactly what it would mean. Grabbing the whistle with one hand and the tiller ropes with the other he blew three blasts signalling distress while there still was enough pressure in the boiler and brought the steamer around to head for the nearest point of land. He knew his position was about two to two and

The sidewheeler *City of Norwich* found herself between the threat of fire and that of water after a collision on Long Island Sound on April 18, 1866. If not for the well-disciplined captain and crew of the steamer and the good fortune that brought another steamer to the scene, the loss of life could easily have exceeded that of the *Lexington* disaster of 1840. *Photo courtesy of Peabody Museum, Salem.*

one-half miles off Huntington, Long Island and he also knew his chances for making it to shallow water were slim. As if to confirm his thoughts the steamer immediately became unmanageable and the water level reached and made inoperative the main boiler. To compound the problem, the water rising in the engine room reached the lower furnace and forced the flames into the fire room igniting the dry woodwork.

As only a fire can race through a dry wooden steamboat, so went this fire, and within ten minutes the perilous situation of the sinking *City of Norwich* was multiplied tenfold. Choking fumes preceded hungry flames through every corridor and into every stateroom and even into the pilothouse. The panic and confusion among the passengers and crew alike was unimaginable. Several passengers, apparently unaware of the still chilly temperature of the sound, immediately leaped overboard to escape the pursuing flames only to find themselves in an equally drastic predicament. A small group of prudent crewmen and passengers managed to gain control of one of the steamer's boats and lowered it properly to the water but within minutes the half frozen and fear-crazed swimmers in their frenzied attempts to clamber aboard managed to capsize the small and overcrowded boat and its usefulness was lost.

The scene all about was incredible. Boxes of freight and pieces of the steamer were floating about like miniature torches giving the appearance of a village that has been pillaged and burned. Things looked very bad for the *City of Norwich* when suddenly, above the roar of the fire and cries of the passengers, Mr. Tracy heard the unmistakeable shrill of a steamboat whistle. Luck was about to turn in their favor.

The steamer *Electra* had been steaming down the sound in the wake of the now burning ship and as soon as the signal of distress had been heard she poured on the coal and sped to the scene of the disaster to render all assistance possible. Captain Nye, of the *Electra*, was a prudent man, however, and the mass of burning debris floating around the burning steamer posed a threat to his vessel as well if he was unwise enough to venture too close. When about three hundred yards from the distressed ship Captain Nye stopped his craft and immediately lowered two boats manned by experienced crewmen to pull to the burning wreck and save as many lives as possible. He was indeed fortunate that two members of his crew had extensive experience with this type of disaster having been survivors from the *Lexington* fire of 1840. He placed each of these men in charge of a boat and had faith that they would be able to do as much as any men could do in this situation.

Navigating among the burning debris was a task in itself but with a strong determination and knowledge of these circumstances the process of saving lives was begun. On board the *Electra* a group of passengers convinced Captain Nye that they could handle another boat to aid in the rescue and he gratefully complied. The job of life saving took quite a while as the blaze continued but when all the survivors reached the *Electra* and a tally was taken it was found that only ten souls were lost. The men of the *Electra* continued searching among the floating debris in hopes of finding further survivors or at least recovering the unfortunates' bodies, but to no avail. With a tremendous hiss and a massive cloud of steam vapor the *City of Norwich* settled into its watery grave in ten fathoms of water. In the excitement, several other vessels of various sizes had arrived on the scene and it was then that Captain Nye discovered that the schooner which had caused the accident was the *Gen. S. Van Vlient* and that it had paid the ultimate price for its misjudgment—it too now lay on the sea floor at the bottom of Long Island Sound. Many passengers learned that day what every mariner fears most of all: fire at sea.

Ten fathoms, sixty feet, is an almost ideal depth for any wreck and despite the fact that this steamer burned considerably the bones that she has undoubtedly left on the bottom are more than worth searching for. Ambitious divers—here's your chance for a good one!

THE *T. A. SCOTT, JR.*

For some strange and unknown reason, shipwrecks of an early vintage, eighteenth or nineteenth century, always seem to have a greater appeal to shipwreck enthusiasts. Perhaps this is because the challenge of tracing a marine disaster which is displaced from us by a considerable period of time is much more difficult and rewarding. Marine disasters of the twentieth century can be equally appealing and often the story behind such a disaster can be even more fascinating. Such is definitely true in the case of the tug T. A. Scott, Jr.

On May 7, 1915 a major historical event of importance to the United States took place at a distance of well over two thousand miles outside our territorial limits. This incident was the deliberate sinking of the British steamer *Lusitania* with a loss of one hundred and twenty-four American lives. History tells us that this was one of the important factors that led to the American entrance into the First World War. Oddly enough considering the ill feeling toward the Central Powers on our part, a German submarine was peacefully visiting an American port over a year and a half later, only months before the United States declared war against that country. The German submarine *Deutschland* hailed from Bremen, Germany, and the exact purpose of her visit here is of little importance to us.

At 1:00 A.M. on November 17, 1916 the submersible fired up her engine while at her temporary berth at New London on the Thames River. It may seem odd that it was leaving the country at such an unusual hour but in fact it was not surprising considering the secretive manner in which the entire trip had been organized and executed. The *Deutschland's* escorts to the open sea were two American tugs of the T. A. Scott Wrecking Company, the *Cassie* and the *T. A. Scott, Jr.* Soon after the tugs arrived at the Eastward Forwarding Company's pier, where the

Pictured is the steam tug *Saturn,* which is similar in many respects to the ill fated *T. A. Scott, Jr.,* which was lost in collision with the German submarine *Deutschland* when both were caught in an eddy off "The Race" in Long Island Sound on November 17, 1916. So sudden was the disaster that all hands except one on the tug were lost. *Photo courtesy of Peabody Museum, Salem.*

submarine was docked, the little convoy set off on their journey down the Thames and across Long Island Sound to a point off Montauk, Long Island where they would part company. There was an uneasy feeling in the air as neither the Americans nor the Germans had much to say to each other—it was not exactly a bon voyage sendoff.

Cruising down the river was a routine procedure for the tugboat captains and was accomplished without any major incidents. Along the way a small launch filled with eager newspaper men picked up the convoy's trail but followed for only a few miles. At the mouth of the river everything appeared calm and quiet. It was a starry night and the sea appeared almost flat for late Fall but this did not upset the men aboard the tugs one little bit. Many a rough trip in November would more than make up for one smooth one. Past the west end of Fisher's Island the ship and tugs proceeded now travelling at a good pace of about twelve knots. A formation had been arranged earlier and was being carried out to the letter. In front, the *Deutschland* and the *Scott* ran almost abreast of one another while half a mile behind the *Cassie* brought up the rear. The scene observed from the *Cassie* was almost eerie. The *Scott* proceeded with her usual running lights posted while the sub was visible only by its single headlight and two side lights. Everything was continuing according to plan.

Suddenly, without warning, at a spot almost seven miles west of Race Rock (at the west end of Fisher's Island) the *Scott* and the *Deutschland* struck a freak eddy (a circular flowing current which is usually of considerable velocity). As those aboard the *Cassie* watched, the tug and submarine were thrown about like toy boats in an angry sea. Then there was a thundering crash followed quickly by an explosion heard as far away as the *Cassie*, still in her regular position in the formation. Captain Baker, her master, didn't need to be told what had happened. He shifted the throttle control full ahead and sped to the scene of the collision expecting the worst and that is exactly what he found. The *T. A. Scott, Jr.* was nowhere to be seen! Apparently, the combination of the strong eddy and the tide running full at the time had thrown the two vessels together with such violence that the *Scott* was forced under almost immediately by the weight of the sub. The explosion heard was caused by the cold water of the sound running in and around the tugboat's boiler. According to a member of the *Deutschland's* crew his vessel struck the tug in the stern with such violence that it lifted its stern right out of water and forced its bow completely under water. The tug *T. A. Scott, Jr.* settled to the bottom of Long Island Sound twelve miles from New London on that cold and clear morning of November 17, 1916 carrying five of her crew of six to their death. In the water, Captain Fred Hinsch, the sole survivor of the *Scott*, struggled against the cold and the overpowering urge to stop struggling and rest until he was plucked from the water to safety.

Both the *Cassie* and the *Deutschland* returned to New London to make sure that the submarine was fit for the trans-Atlantic voyage still ahead and to make sure that all the paper work regarding this incident was rapidly and correctly completed. During the next few days the shipbuilding inspectors were allowed to see the external damage but none were allowed aboard the sub. Repairs were eventually made and finally, with a little more secrecy and a little less notoriety, the German submarine *Deutschland* set sail for her homeland again.

What became of the *Deutschland?* Who knows? What became of the *T. A. Scott, Jr.?* As far as is known it might very well still be lying on the bottom of Long Island Sound (maybe it's even in an upright position!). Have at it!

14 New York

THE *LEXINGTON*

NEW York City, perhaps the largest trading center of every imaginable type of goods in the world, has held the number one position in terms of important east coast ports almost exclusively since the early days of our country's history. The shipping routes to and from the city have changed only slightly over the years: entrance from southern ports is via New York Harbor and from northern ports is via Long Island Sound and the East River. As we have seen, even in the early and mid-nineteenth century years, the marine traffic traveling to and from New York was extensive making the trip a dangerous one and even more so at night.

The steam side-wheeler *Lexington* was one of numerous vessels which sailed these waters on a regular basis. Originally built in 1835 by Brown & Bell, the *Lexington* was first owned by Cornelius Vanderbilt who paid the exhorbitant price of $110,000 for what was acclaimed as the finest boat on the sound in its day. She was built of the finest materials: oak, cedar, chestnut, and yellow and white pine. In addition, she was butt bolted with iron bolts and boasted thirty per cent more fastenings than any other boat on the sound. She measured two hundred and five feet from stem to stern post, was twenty-two feet of beam (with a measurement of forty-six feet between the outsides of the wheel guards) and displaced in the area of four hundred tons. When Vanderbilt decided to sell the Lexington he had no trouble finding a buyer. Her record stood behind her: a long and safe history of running on the sound. The New Jersey Steam Navigation and Transportation Company bought the steamer for $60,060 and decided to continue to run the well known vessel on her normal New York to Stonington route.

Like many ships of the day the *Lexington* was run with little or no insurance, an unwise practice adopted by many ship owners. The steamer

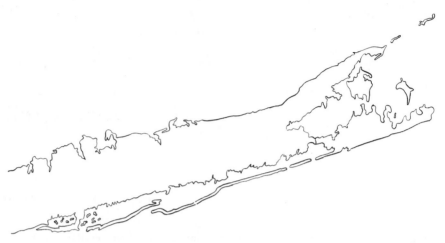

carried no marine insurance at all and only $20,000 worth of fire insurance. Who would know the price to be paid for that oversight? In November of 1839 the side-wheeler was hauled on the marine railway and thoroughly examined and repaired. This was often the practice with ship owners prior to running their vessels through the winter when the threat of ice against an old or insecure hull was ominous. At this time, in addition to checking her bottom, replacing worn or missing pieces of coppering, and inspecting her boilers, machinery and furnaces, the *Lexington* was converted from a wood burner to a coal burning steamer. This meant less time and money would be spent in aquiring and storing logwood aboard which would also leave more space for extra freight.

Before this overhaul was finished the local United States Steamboat Inspector, Elihu S. Bunker, issued a certificate of soundness and seaworthiness. Safety equipment and safe construction were also a strong point of this gallant side-wheeler: 1) the boiler was in the hold, almost eighteen inches from the floor timber, and under it was a lining of bricks and a cast iron pan with water in case of fire; 2) an outside coating had been constructed around the smoke stack with an eight inch space between the outer coating and the pipe; under normal conditions this space would be steam filled, thus precluding the chance of sparks flying from the stack to any woodwork nearby; 3) iron steering rods were used rather than ropes which might become twisted or, in case of fire, might burn off; 4) it was directed that no exposed woodwork should be located in the vicinity of the boiler or pipe; 5) three staunch boats were stored in various locations in case abandonment of the ship was necessary; and 6) maybe best of all, the *Lexington* had a brand new fire engine complete with hoses and pumps on board. There was no doubt about it—the crew of the *Lexington* was prepared for any possible mishap. What more could the owners want than a fast, safe and popular boat!

Monday morning, January 13, 1840, found the *Lexington* at her berth in New York, the last bits of general cargo being loaded for the trip to Stonington on the afternoon tide. It would be a pretty crowded trip today, thought Captain Childs as he gazed down from his perch in the pilothouse observing some of his crewmen as they loaded the last of one hundred and fifty bales of cotton on the deck. Much had been stored below deck but it simply would not all fit with seventy-five passengers coming aboard in just a few hours. The day was slightly overcast but there was only a slight breeze to disturb the flat calm of the harbor. If the weather held it would be a comfortable and profitable trip.

By noon, all of the cargo had been stowed aboard and by 2:00 P.M. all the passengers except for a few stragglers were aboard and anxious to

The sidewheel steamer *Lexington* has the distinction of being the victim of the first major steamboat disaster on Long Island Sound. Overcome by a fire that claimed the lives of all but four persons aboard, the steamer drifted about for several hours looking like a floating torch until she sunk off Old Field Point, Long Island, on January 13, 1840. *Photo courtesy of Peabody Museum, Salem.*

leave but, true to form, Captain Childs would blow his whistle and cast off his lines at his regular departure time of 3:00 P.M. The trip down the East River to the head of the sound was always the most dangerous part of the journey as the river was narrow and heavily traveled. As he had hoped, the captain found the sound to be almost dead calm and after leaving the river he turned over command of the pilothouse to the mate and went below to dine with some of his passengers. The captain always enjoyed this practice as it broke up the monotony of the regular ten or twelve hour run between Stonington and New York.

For the next two hours everything proceeded normally until just after 7:00 P.M. when the mate sent for the captain to come up to the pilothouse. This was extremely unusual and Captain Childs wasted no time in complying. Upon his arrival in the pilothouse the mate informed him that there was a problem below with a fire and he had thought it best to quietly alert the master so as not to cause alarm. Captain Childs agreed completely and sent his mate below to see that the incident might be corrected immediately. Before the mate had left the pilothouse the steamer's direction was altered to head her toward the Long Island shore. Captain Childs was taking no chances. At that time the *Lexington* was approximately two miles to the eastward of Eaton's Neck Light. With luck they would make the shore in about fifteen minutes if that was found to be necessary but, deep inside, the captain hoped that the problem would be nothing but a minor one, one which his able crew could handle with dispatch. Little could he guess the horrifying night that lay ahead for everyone aboard the ill-fated steamer. Minutes passed like hours as the captain patiently awaited the return of his mate with the word that the new fire engine had done its job.

Suddenly, he heard the cry that he had dearly hoped not to hear: *fire!* The very last thing that he needed at that moment was seventy-five screaming and panic-stricken passengers running in all directions at once. Captain Hilliard, a passenger, who was a very qualified and intelligent master of his own ship, had been conversing with Captain Childs earlier and upon hearing the alarm of fire knew instinctively that Captain Childs would need all the assistance he could get. He rushed out on the promenade deck just in time to see flames pouring out of the woodwork around the chimney. He made his way with difficulty to the pilothouse to advise his friend to head for the shore as quickly as he could, only to learn that the *Lexington's* captain had been doing so for several minutes.

Below decks, Mr. Crowley, the Second Mate, discovered six bales of cotton on fire and this fire was rapidly spreading to the woodwork. He quickly summoned all available hands including Captain Manchester, the

Pilot, and handed back three water buckets to be filled and then thrown at the blaze in an effort to quench the hungry flames. The volunteer firefighters continued in this manner until the flames and smoke drove them back. In the meantime, several panicking passengers and some crewmen were trying to launch the ship's boats as quickly as possible. In their panic, the crewmen and the passengers failed to realize that the steamer was still under way and the first boat lowered quickly capsized, filled with water, and even worse, as the captain watched from the pilothouse, struck the paddle wheel and was lost. Likewise, a second attempt was taking place on the other side of the steamer and, although this boat missed being destroyed by the paddle wheel, it drifted off, full of passengers, never to be seen again.

As if there weren't enough problems the engine at that moment ceased running and the gallant *Lexington* became a floating torch on Long Island Sound. The third boat was in the process of being launched as Captain Childs left the pilothouse in an effort to make his way aft to try and calm the frenzied crowd. He spotted the last boat leaving the ship and made an instantaneous decision to try to comandeer it and help save as many persons as possible but, as he approached the boat, the line attaching it to the *Lexington* was cut and it began to drift off into the night. With a valiant effort Captain Childs leaped for the boat and successfully reached its bow. That boat was gone in an instant and, like the other two, would never be seen or heard of again.

There is no word to describe the activity on board the rapidly burning ship short of chaos. Within five minutes after the engine stopped the smoke from the roaring flames was so dense that all communication between the forward and aft portions of the ship were cut off. Captain Hilliard became the focal point around which the passengers rallied. Their fear and panic was so intense at this point that they didn't know what to do or where to go to escape the fate of death by burning on the ship or the fate of death by drowning or exposure from the forty degree water. The figure of Captain Hilliard helped instill some confidence in the passengers that there was some hope although all knew that they could not stay aboard the *Lexington*. At his orders, the passengers and remaining crewmen began throwing overboard anything and everything that would float (cotton bales, crates, etc.) so that each would have something upon which to support himself when he deserted the burning steamer.

Charles Smith, a deckhand, left his ship at about 8:00 P.M. and swam to a cotton bale upon which he proceeded to save himself. Meanwhile, at the forward end of the steamer, someone suggested building a raft and everyone there seemed to think that was a good idea. All pitched in and began to tear apart any crates or other wooden objects they could find to piece together a floatable platform. Unfortunately, as they were working on a method of joining the pieces, the fire proceeded, under the deck, to travel forward and the deck quickly became so intolerably hot that all in the forward section were forced to abandon ship and hope that they could find some piece of floating wreckage to cling to in hopes of preserving their lives.

Around the peripheral areas of the steamer small groups of frightened passengers found shelter as they could—on the braces, under the guards, and on the outer edges of the rail—until, one by one, they were forced to jump into the bone-chilling sea or risk being roasted alive. Captain Hilliard, in much the same manner as Charles Smith, left the ship on a bale of cotton and floated in the vicinity of the "floating bonfire" for several hours.

The men of the sloop *Merchant*, of Southport, under the command of Captain Meeker, were the first to spot the perilous position of those aboard the blazing steamer but in attempting to leave the harbor ran hard aground on the bar in a falling tide and were forced to remain there until the next morning and a rising tide before they could continue on their mission of mercy. The sky remained cloudy making the burning steamer an awesome sight until about 9:00 P.M. when it became a very clear and cold night. As the passengers and crewmen floated around in the freezing water of the sound the paradox of the heat of the blaze and the coldness of the water must have been an anguishing one, indeed.

Captain Manchester, the Pilot, was one of the few persons who remained safely aboard the steamer until midnight when he spotted and made good use of a floating bale of cotton. Charles Smith, the deckhand, brought his bale of cotton back near the ship at about 1:30 A.M. after drifting around for about five and one half hours. Many passengers and crewmen had perished by this time. Smith had a good idea and tied his cotton bale to the ship so that he might have the safety of the cotton bale while sharing some of the heat from the fire. This worked pretty well until the Lexington made her final plunge, about 3:00 A.M., and with a sudden unexpectedness Smith lost his bale of cotton which had to be replaced by a charred piece of wreckage.

Those who survived the night were well qualified to express what true suffering is; many more perished than survived. With the dawn came hope for the few remaining survivors but they all found themselves drifting to different parts of the sound. It would be a miracle if any of them lived to tell the story. Captain Hilliard's account of that fearful night serves as a good example of what all went through during those freezing hours on and off their precious bales or pieces of wreckage in each man's effort to battle the elements and win. He told of using a piece of wreckage as a paddle in an effort to force his bale to travel in the direction of the nearest shore but as fate would have it the same falling tide that prevented the Merchant from succeeding in her rescue attempt also kept the wreckage from drifting towards shore. After several dunkings from trying to determine the best method of straddling a bale of cotton the captain gave up and decided to rest on the bale making as few movements as possible so that the bale might not treat him to another freezing salt water bath. By and by, with the sunrise, he managed to dry himself out a little which made things much more comfortable.

At about 9:00 A.M. the Merchant freed itself of its sandy anchor and proceeded with all haste to the scene of the disaster to search for survivors. Captain Hilliard was the first to be picked up at about 11:00 A.M. He was so numbed from exposure that he could hardly speak but when he spotted a sail coming toward him he rallied and managed to attract the attention of the men aboard the sloop by waving his handkerchief. The men aboard the sloop were concerned as to what ship had been lost but the captain was so insensible that he could not reply to their questions with coherent answers.

The search continued and later in the day Captain Manchester and Charles Smith were picked up, both alive, if not well. Out of a crew of thirty-five and a passenger list of seventy-five had only three men survived the conflagration? The *Merchant* continued to search after having stopped a passing steamer bound for New York to send the news and the survivors there for further medical care.

When the news reached New York, and almost immediately thereafter Stonington, the city was aghast. Who had been aboard? Where were the bodies for identification? How could such a catastrophe happen? Never in the brief history of American steam navigation had such a disaster occurred. An immediate effort had to be made to save any further lives and property. The owners of the steamer *Statesman* volunteered the use of their vessel and a volunteer crew was hastily assembled. Before a full day had passed since the fire, the *Statesman* set out with the intention of searching the entire length of shoreline of Long Island from Huntington to Fresh Pond Landing. This would be quite a task as its length, when considering all the inlets and bays, would be nearly ninety miles. The plan was for the Statesman to leave groups of searchers at designated spots inaccessible to the ship who would be picked up further down the shore.

The search went much more slowly than expected as the cold weather caused numerous problems with ice along the shore to say nothing of the drift ice in the sound which the *Statesman* must carefully navigate around. Wreckage began to turn up on the shore between Crane's Neck and Old Man's Landing but no news of further survivors or bodies was heard. The search continued with only remnants of the *Lexington* being found and as the week wore on the volunteers grew restless to get back to their regular jobs.

A rumor was picked up on Thursday morning that a man had made his way ashore at River Head, nearly forty miles west of the scene of the disaster. Several of the rescuers scoffed at the idea as being absurd but the rumor had to be checked out. Unbelievably enough, David Crowley, the Second Mate of the *Lexington,* had survived for two days and two nights aboard a bale of cotton and then managed to reach the safety of a local resident's home.

There would be no more survivors found! The statistic was staggering—of those who boarded the *Lexington* on Monday less than four per cent survived. An inquest into the disaster began shortly thereafter and many facts of interest came to light. Of major importance to all was the cause of the disaster. After several experts testified as to the safety of burning coal for fuel rather than wood and other experts related details of all of the safety precautions already mentioned, the following conclusions were made: 1) several bales of cotton were, in fact, stored too close to the smoke stack for safety; 2) it was probably here (in the bales of cotton) that the fire began; 3) necessarily, the fire had to have begun below the promenade deck where it was first spotted; and 4) the exact cause of the blaze was proposed to be from the chimney getting red hot (which many said was impossible) and causing the cotton and nearby woodwork to catch fire.

Several experts put their heads together to determine the approximate location of the wreck and it seemed likely that with the tide and wind conditions that prevailed at the time of the disaster the remains would lie approximately four miles north of Old Field Point Light. It came to light at this time that there was a more valuable cargo aboard than had been previously thought. Evidently a Mr. Harnden, of Harnden's Express Company, had been aboard and with him he had bank notes valued at $20,000 and about $18,000 in specie. The bank notes and almost $10,000 in specie were stored in a leather trunk which was lined with iron. The trunk was situated in an iron chest which had been stored in one of the express cars (crates) on the back of the steamer. The reaction to this announcement was quick and predictable—within months several parties would begin to plan attempts to locate the remains and salvage the "treasure."

One other fact worthy of mention was brought out at the inquest: apparently, during the night while the steamer was blazing a sloop, the *Improvement,* was seen to pass the burning ship and in an unbelievable act of inhumanity did nothing to attempt to rescue any survivors. Despite the pleadings of his crew, Captain William Tirrell of the *Improvement* refused to render aid even though he was at one time within a short two miles of the scene. His excuse: if he should stop to render assistance to those aboard the steamer he would miss the tide at his destination and have to wait outside the bar until the next morning to bring his ship into the harbor. Public reaction to this act of extremely bad conduct was severe. Captain Tirrell was lucky to retain his master's papers.

Now, let's jump ahead a little bit. In September of 1842 one of the ambitious teams of treasure hunters did, in fact, locate the remains of the *Lexington.* How or why they decided to raise the entire hull of the vessel is unclear but in any event they did. The once gallant steamer was destined to see the sunlight again if only for a few moments before the chains supporting her bones snapped and dumped the proud side-wheeler back to the bottom again. The depth of the water where she was located is just over one hundred feet, which definitely does not put this wreck out of the reach of modern day wreck searchers. Incidentally, the salvagers that managed to raise the hull (at least temporarily) did receive some treasure for their efforts—a thirty pound lump of silver valued at about $800. This is important to take note of, for in the frenzy of the burning ship we know that many things were thrown over to serve as life preservers. It would have seemed likely that Herndon's chest received similar treatment—but the lump of melted silver was recovered from the location of the hull itself. One other salvage attempt was made on the wreck but was abandoned. Maybe on the bottom of Long Island Sound off Old Field's Point there is a melted lump of silver waiting for you!

THE *ENTERPRISE*

Fisher's Island, New York, is a small rocky refuge, only seven miles long and no more than two miles wide at its widest point. Lying off the coast of Rhode Island and Connecticut its western extremity stands as one half of the entrance to Long Island Sound. The dangers at the easterly end of the island have already been mentioned and the western end poses equally great danger from "The Race" where exceptionally strong current is the rule rather than the exception. The southern shoreline which represents the ocean side of the island would naturally be more rugged than the leeward side and also has a greater percentage of shipwrecks. As with Block Island and the sounds generally, Fisher's Island is frequently subject to dense fog banks which make the trip through the sound a tricky one.

Under just this set of weather conditions the little steamer *Enterprise* was lost on the shore of Fisher's Island on May 26, 1874. Like many other steamers of her day the *Enterprise* regularly traveled between Providence and New York. She was primarily a cargo carrier rather than a passenger steamer but often carried both.

On her voyage to destiny she was travelling southward having left her berth in Providence on Monday, May 25th. Her cargo consisted mainly of railroad iron and a huge punching machine under consignment to the Brooklyn Navy Yard. As the *Enterprise* steamed along the southern coast of Rhode Island in the dense fog of the early morning her master, Captain Dibble, used extreme caution, proceeding slowly and sounding his ship's shrill whistle continually. The last thing that Captain Dibble wanted was to encounter another ship in the fog and he hugged the shore which seemed the prudent thing to do at the time. Actually, he was about to learn that his decision had not been wise at all.

Just after 6:00 A.M. the Mate heard a slight thump and the *Enterprise* came to a gentle halt. So quiet was the mishap that it was several minutes before all of the crewmen knew that something was wrong. The sea was calm and the wind a mere breeze as the captain and his crew met on deck to figure out exactly what had happened and more important where they were. It took some doing but the men finally decided that they were near Watch Hill or Fisher's Island. Their predicament became more dangerous with each hour as the wind and surf picked up and before long the captain felt that it would be best if they all left the ship for the shelter of the shore. Without incident, the ship's complement reached the shore and set out to find out exactly where they were. In short order, they discovered that they had landed on the south shore of Fisher's Island near the eastern end. There were few residents living on Fisher's Island in 1874 and communication with the mainland was anything but regular. Thus, Captain Dibble found himself and his steamer in a predicament until a small boat could be acquired to take at least one man to the mainland to notify the owners and a wrecking crew in hopes that the *Enterprise* could be hauled off undamaged.

On May 26, 1874, the steamer *Enterprise* quietly ran ashore on the south side of Fisher's Island in Long Island Sound. Despite the gentleness of the stranding, and due in part to the remoteness of the location of the accident from the professional salvagers, the steamer was lost as she lay. Pictured is the steamer *Middletown*, of similar construction. *Photo courtesy of Peabody Museum, Salem.*

As he watched from the shore Captain Dibble saw his fine steamer turn broadside to the beach and as the sea intensified the waves began crashing over the vessel with the sole intent of claiming her bones. Unknown to Captain Dibble the predicament of the *Enterprise* had been spotted by a passing steamer whose captain immediately reported her location and apparent condition upon his arrival at port. Scott, the wrecker, had been notified late on the 26th and immediately put his men to work preparing one of his wrecking schooners for the trip to Fisher's Island. On the morning of May 27th from the beach it appeared the *Enterprise's* condition was rapidly becoming hopeless. As the captain and his mate surveyed the situation they were surprised and pleased to hear that

Captain Scott had just arrived on the island and would be at the site shortly.

Scott's appraisal of the situation was not what Captain Dibble had hoped for. Scott had a vast knowledge of wrecking and of the most dangerous spots in the vicinity. He related that the steamer was lying in an exposed position on a bed of rocks which would, if calm weather did not return immediately, pound the bottom right out of the little steamer. Once the bottom was gone the vessel would lose its ability to give with the waves and it would become a large pile of splinters in short order. The sea abated somewhat over the next few days and the steamer put up a staunch fight for survival but in the end all that Scott could save was the valuable punching machine, which had been lashed to the deck because of its size and bulk, and a portion of the ship's steam engine. Once again the power of the sea had proved that it deserved respect as the uninsured $20,000 steamer became an almost total loss.

The statistics of the *Enterprise* were as follows: she was built in Saco, Maine in 1866 of the best local timbers available and measured one hundred and eighteen feet in length by twenty feet of beam and drew over eight feet of water when light. Her registered tonnage was two hundred and five gross tons and she was owned by Captain Towne, of New York, and Mr. R. F. Hartley, of Biddeford, Maine.

Searching for this wreck might not be as difficult as you might suspect. Being very heavily laden at the time of her stranding she was probably drawing at least twelve feet of water at the time. This gives a basic starting point for a search in terms of the depth of water. Also, her cargo of railroad iron was, as far as we know, unsalvaged which means that in the immediate vicinity of the wreck there must be a large pile of iron. Combining these two facts and utilizing an underwater sled the problem of locating the remains of the *Enterprise* might be an easy task, indeed!

THE *WILLIAM MALONEY*

There have been many hundreds of thousands of shipwrecks throughout man's written history—strandings, sinkings, founderings, collisions, etc. Perhaps the least enviable of all types of marine disasters is the small catagory headed "Lost at Sea." A confirmed disaster is one thing, with survivors or spectators to relate the details of what happened and what caused it to happen. Being lost, however, brings out a fear of the unknown in all men. To know that a ship has been lost and yet have no

On November 15, 1924, the tug *William Maloney* left her berth at Newton Creek in Brooklyn, New York, to steam to Newport, R.I., in search of work. Somewhere along the way, perhaps in the storm of the sixteenth on Long Island Sound, the tug disappeared without a trace. The *Julia C. Moran* is representative of small tugs of this era. *Photo courtesy of Peabody Museum, Salem.*

information concerning exactly where or why fate has chosen to pluck out a vessel and the lives of those aboard is perplexing at best.

The loss of the steam tug *William Maloney* is a fascinating story. There are many strange and inconsistent facts which lead to many unanswered questions. The *Maloney* was a medium sized tug of about one hundred and sixty-five gross tons built of wood in Yarmouth, Nova Scotia in 1891. She was steam powered and screw driven and, when new, had an appraised value of about $5,000. Apparently, she was owned by either Jacob Aaron or John L. Leechan of New York and either Aaron or Charles Cox acted in the capacity of master. Her home port was New York or New London but it seems that she took contracts for jobs as far away as Rhode Island. Her dimensions have been elusive to this point but she must have been a fairly large vessel as she required a total crew of twelve men. On November 15, 1924 the William Maloney was preparing to leave the port of Newton Creek, Brooklyn, New York bound up the sounds to Newport (or Providence), Rhode Island for a job. Somewhere in Long Island Sound or Block Island Sound the steam tug apparently sunk as there was a severe storm in the vicinity of Long Island on November 15th and 16th. This in itself is not strange or unusual—ships have been sinking for hundreds of years.

The unusual nature of the story is to be discerned in the innumerable and unexplainable twists. First, of all, apparently no one in Newport got worried when the Maloney failed to show up. No attempt at communication was made with the tug's owner and the incident was simply dropped. The Coast Guard was for some reason not notified of the overdue vessel and no alarm or search was ever initiated. In fact, until the following January it seemed that no one could care less what might have happened to the *Maloney* or its crew. The first to express an interest was a relative of one of the crewmen who was interested in some official confirmation of the rumor that the little tug had been lost so that she might be able to collect on an insurance claim. It seemed that it took an excessive amount of work to make the Coast Guard inquire into the disaster for it was the following February before an inquiry was addressed to the New York office of the Customs Service concerning the tug. The reply to this inquiry was unbelievable. After checking locally, the Customs Service people replied that they were unable to find any person at that port who was interested in the vessel. An inquiry addressed to the owner of the *Maloney* (Aaron or Leechman?) was returned by the Postmaster as undeliverable. Since all inquiry concerning the loss of the tug was insurance-related the Coast Guard let the case drop without ever holding even a preliminary investigation! By late in 1927 the entire incident had been settled and forgotten. From what can be surmised now there was never any reported wreckage from the wreck and no bodies ever washed up on a beach to be identified as one of the twelve who mysteriously disappeared.

It would be sheer conjecture to make a guess at the precise location of this wreck. This, however, does not mean that the *Maloney* is unlocatable. Probably the best procedure to follow would be to gather all the pertinent facts available concerning the storm, the normal route travelled from Newton Creek to Newport and exact information on the speed capability of the tug. By setting up a timetable of events keeping in mind the weather and the ship's potential headway under these conditions the search area for the wreck could be probably pinpointed to within about ten miles. A close check of local newspapers might turn up a small account of wreckage ashore to assist in reducing this search area. It would be an extremely long and arduous task to locate the remains of the *William Maloney* but there is little doubt in my mind that it could, in fact, be accomplished and probably with very rewarding results.

This ends a brief discussion of the possibilities available to the ambitious wreck searcher but this should not be considered to be the end. I have tried to express one major thought throughout this work: that there are shipwrecks everywhere there is water. Sure it will take a lot of time and tremendous effort to locate the better wrecks, but I cannot express just how worthwhile it will be. Do it now!

Index